You're an animal! It doesn't matter how expensive your trainers are, how much deodorant you use or how big a car your folks own – you're still an animal. We're all animals. OK, we don't sniff each others' bottoms when we meet and we don't live in holes in the ground, but we're still animals.

You'd think, in that case, we would be a bit more understanding before hurling insults at people – 'you're a beast', 'you're a brute', 'you're an animal'. I wonder if animals ever think, in their own way, that 'you're nothing but a human' is an insult? They should do because the damage we've done to animals and the world is much greater than anything they have ever done.

Juliet Gellatley has spent most of her life campaigning for animal rights. After taking a degree in zoology, she rose to become the Vegetarian Society's Director. In 1994, she launched Viva!, the vegetarian and animal charity for adults and young people. She is the winner of the first Linda McCartney Award for Animal Welfare and the author of *The Livewire Guide to Going, Being and Staying Veggie!* (Livewire, 1996) and *The Silent Ark*.

Juliet Gellatley

Born to be Wild

The Livewire Guide to Saving Animals

Livewire

from The Women's Press

First published by Livewire Books, The Women's Press Ltd, 2000
A member of the Namara Group
34 Great Sutton Street, London EC1V 0LQ
www.the-womens-press.com

Reprinted 2001

British Library Cataloguing-in-Publication Data
A catalogue record for this book is available from the British Library.

ISBN 0 7043 4969 8

Typeset in 12/14pt Bembo by FiSH Books, London
Printed and bound in Great Britain by Cox & Wyman, Reading,
Berkshire

For Charlie – don't you bite my nose!

And for Tony, Jo, Lesley, Fi, Becky, Kate, Graeme, John and Greg – the Viva! team supremos who work so hard for the animals. Also to Audrey, John and Paul for making so much of our work possible.

Finally for Lulu, Jazzy, Teatime and Tishy for their humour, passion and love – and all the animals in the world who deserve so much more from the human race. One day we'll learn to respect this wonderful and precious world instead of robbing it of all that is beautiful.

Contents

Introduction   1

Chapter 1 Fashion Without Compassion:
Animals Killed for Fur and Leather   8

Chapter 2 Killing for Kicks:
Hunting and Fighting Animals for Pleasure   22

Chapter 3 Under Fire:
Hunting Animals for Profit   45

Chapter 4 Behind Bars:
Animals in Zoos and Circuses   65

Chapter 5 Blinded by Science:
Experiments on Animals   83

Chapter 6 Creature Comforts:
Companion Animals at Home   101

Chapter 7 Animal Farm:
The Life of Farmed Animals   122

Chapter 8 The Killing Fields:
The Live Export and Slaughter of Farmed Animals   149

Chapter 9 Hook, Line and Sinker:
Killing Fish for Fun and Food   170

Chapter 10 Frankenstein Foods:
The Genetic Engineering of Animals   187

Chapter 11 In the Name of God:
Animals and Religion   202

Chapter 12 Close to the Edge:
Animals on the Brink of Extinction   215

Conclusion: Why Does it Matter?   231

Directory of Animal Groups   241

Index   258

Introduction

You're an animal! It doesn't matter how expensive your trainers, how much deodorant you use or how big a car your folks own – you're still an animal. We're all animals. OK, we don't sniff each others' bottoms when we meet and we don't live in holes in the ground, but we're still animals.

You'd think, in that case, we would be a bit more understanding before hurling insults at people – 'you're a beast', 'you're a brute', 'you're an animal'. I wonder if animals ever think, in their own way, that 'you're nothing but a human' is an insult? They should do because the damage we've done to animals and the world is much greater than anything they have ever done. Our cruelty to animals is so widespread and so vast it's almost impossible to take in.

The crazy thing is, we choose which animals we want to abuse and those we don't and it varies from country to country. Try and make sense out of this. In the West we adore cats and dogs, feed them, house them and spend huge amounts of money on them when they're ill. When

1

they die we miss them and mourn them because they were our friends. Even while we're still grieving, we might eat a hamburger (well, not me) without giving a thought to the poor cow who was slaughtered for its meat. On the other hand, in Asia some people eat cats and dogs and think nothing of it.

Walk through the countryside and you'll hear birds singing away to their hearts' content. We have laws to protect songbirds. But the ducks you feed on the village pond, beautiful pheasants, partridge, woodcock and snipe – all glorious, harmless creatures – have almost no protection and some people blast them out of the sky with shotguns and call it sport. If it's a crow, rook or magpie, you can kill it whenever you like, even when it's sitting on its nest. They're 'pests', you see!

The truth is that humans have used other animals for our own ends since we first evolved a couple of million years ago, even though we were all originally vegetarian. As we spread out from our original home in Africa, we became opportunists – we ate whatever was available. We killed animals for their meat and used their skins for clothing and shelter. Later, we became farmers and tamed wild animals, domesticating them so we could keep them in fields close at hand for when we wanted to kill them. We used them as beasts of burden – to transport us and our goods, to haul timber and stone and to plough our fields.

The more that humans developed, the more they exploited animals. They shot lions and tigers for fun, harpooned whales and netted just about every creature in the sea. Birds were imprisoned in tiny cages to entertain them with their singing or mimicking. Anything that fed on their crops was trapped, poisoned or shot. As villages developed into cities and people had no land, they had to be provided with food as well as everything else they needed. And so the exploitation really began to take off – because money was involved.

Millions of beautiful wild creatures were cruelly trapped for their fur to make into coats. Others were caged in zoos – for our education, they said. Just as bad, some were turned into nothing more than sideshows, made to perform for paying customers in circuses. Cruelties such as tearing foxes and badgers to pieces with dogs was another entertainment. But is this any worse, I wonder, than torturing to death millions of animals for something called vivisection – ie medical experiments or to test cosmetics or oven cleaners?

This, better than anything else, shows our attitude to animals. It's perfectly OK to inflict terrible suffering on an innocent creature, who has no idea what is happening to it or why, in order – they claim – to save us from suffering. We count and they don't.

One distressing scene that took place less than 100 years ago just about sums up how some people have no concern for animal suffering. A man called Thomas Eddison invented a way of killing with electricity and wanted it to become the official American way of executing criminals. He wanted to demonstrate to government officials just how effective a method it was. So he electrocuted an elephant at a public exhibition.

The massive creature refused to die and bellowed in pain and terror, so Eddison kept giving it shock after shock until he eventually brought it down, still bellowing, its flesh burning. No one expressed one word of concern for the elephant and the electric chair came into being. Since then, people have been so horrified at this cruelty that the film of the elephant's death is never shown.

Animals were on this Earth long before humans. They began to evolve 3,500 million years ago and spread to every corner of the globe. Some developed in very special ways.

Take the poor old mole rat. If you were to hold a popularity contest for the prettiest, cuddliest and most appealing animal in the world, it wouldn't be the mole rat. It is hairless and blind and spends its entire life underground eating worms and slugs. It doesn't even like other mole rats and has nothing to do with them, except once a year when it finds a partner and mates.

On the other hand, the cheetah might top the vote for most beautiful animal. It is one of the fastest on earth and can run at 70 mph. It only does so in short bursts, when it chases its dinner. And that dinner is usually a Tompson's gazelle, which can match the cheetah stride for stride – almost.

The Tompson's gazelle grazes on grass and shrubs and eats no meat, while the cheetah is a carnivore and has to eat meat or it will die. Despite the differences, each has become what it is because of the other. The Tompson had to develop its camouflage colouring so it could not be easily seen; it had to be forever watchful so it could see the cheetah's attack coming; and it had to become an extremely fast runner in order to survive. The cheetah had to become faster and faster; it had to be silent and crafty; and it had to blend into the countryside so it also wasn't easily seen and could get close enough to launch its final devastating burst of speed.

Because both animals are so evenly matched, the

Tompsons that tend to get caught are the old, the weak, the very young, the injured and the ill. You can just imagine how little chance a poor old Tompson stands if it's born with poor hearing or sight, or a calf whose mother doesn't hide it in the grass properly. In the same way, a blind or three-legged cheetah doesn't stand much chance of catching anything.

Although this all seems cruel, it plays a vital part in the survival of both species and they both play an important part in their environment – as do all animals, even the poor old mole rat. Only the fittest live to have babies and it is these healthy animals who pass on their genes to the next generation.

When people talk about the survival of the fittest, this is what they mean. But it isn't just about strength, it's about being best fitted to survive. No matter how big and strong an elephant is, if it's born with a short trunk it may not be able to reach as much food as other elephants and may not survive. This is 'natural selection'.

What's important to remember about this is that even those animals who have to kill other animals don't threaten the survival of that species. In fact they help it to survive by preventing it breeding out of control which, if allowed to happen, would lead to the spread of diseases and mass starvation. Predators also help by removing the more sickly animals so that only the fittest are left to breed. That's how it was for millions of years until humans came along.

We have destroyed this natural balance because we believe we are separate and apart from it – that we aren't really animals. In fact, we have turned them into nothing more than mass-products, as if they were shoes or tins of peas.

We claim we are so superior that only humans feel pain and suffering or comfort and happiness. And this becomes an excuse to do terrible things to animals. The Christian church supported it by claiming that animals had no souls, only humans did. This was the same religion that 200 years ago said that black people were not human – they said that because they were animals and had no feelings it was perfectly OK to turn them into slaves.

Throughout history, powerful people have supported many things that damage animals and nature simply because they can make money out of it. This has now gone so far that it is threatening the survival of the planet. A rifle bullet kills anything and everything and plays no part in natural selection. When forests are wiped out, everything in them dies. When seas are overfished, other creatures die because there is no food for them.

It isn't surprising, then, that 75 per cent of all the animals on the planet are disappearing fast and many are facing extinction – and extinction is forever! There is little hope that this will end until we start to face up to the cruelty that we hand out to almost every living creature, just because it suits us.

I founded Viva! in 1994 to expose the most widespread mass cruelty in the world – that of farmed animals. In 1999, 43 billion of them were slaughtered throughout the world. Most had been reared in the most cruel painful conditions imaginable and slaughtered in ways that should shame us. I wanted people to face up to this mass abuse which is happening on a scale that the globe has never witnessed in its entire history.

I admit this makes for some difficult reading. But the need for action has never been greater and that's what

Born to be Wild and Viva! are all about – action for animals.

I have campaigned against all kinds of cruelty and this book records many examples and the excuses that are used to support it. Each chapter in this book begins with a letter from one of Viva!'s young supporters – people who have seen things that have stung them into action to defend animals. By including their observations I hope to bring the issues to life and make them seem real. But *Born to be Wild* isn't just a catalogue of suffering. At the end of each chapter is a list of Success Stories that have been achieved by people who are determined to act. In Action for Animals I detail what you can do to help the fight, together with the organisations that are working for a better world. These are the most important sections of the book. Finally, a comprehensive list of all the organisations – their addresses, emails and websites – are brought together in a comprehensive directory at the back of the book.

I believe that all creatures have a part to play on Earth, and we have to live in harmony with them. If we don't, not only will the animals not survive but neither will we. You can start to put things right by not exploiting animals yourself and encouraging others not to either. We all have to treat animals for what they are – an amazingly beautiful part of our lives that help to make life worth living. It isn't a choice of us or them – it's all of us or nothing.

'The animals of the world exist for their own reasons.
They are not made for humans any more than black
people were made for whites or women for men.'
Alice Walker

7

Chapter 1

Fashion Without Compassion

Animals Killed for Fur and Leather

Danielle Davis, 17, was walking along minding her own business one evening and suddenly found herself involved in a row that changed her life.

'I was on my way home. I guess it must have been about seven thirty, the light was just going and I stopped to have a look in a shop window on the High Street. Right next to me was a café. I wasn't paying any attention but then this woman walked out and everything about her seemed to be saying "look at me look at me, aren't I gorgeous".

'She was waiting for someone and stood on the pavement looking up and down. I was hit by a wave of perfume that could only have drifted from her. She was wearing a coat, holding it closed around her. And what a coat! It almost reached the ground and was fur from top to bottom – thick, silvery fur streaked with flecks of a light reddish colour. She looked like a pop star.

'She was still watching and waiting when this young couple came up to her. The girl asked her a question. She wasn't exactly polite but she wasn't rude either. She said: "Is that real fur?" The woman laughed and said, as if she'd been offended, "Of course it is!" The girl then said, "It's arctic fox, isn't it?"

'The woman obviously thought the girl was interested and she became more chatty saying that it was a present from her husband and cost a lot of money. But the girl's voice suddenly went hard and she said: "Shall I tell you how those poor animals are caught? It's so cruel you should be ashamed of yourself."

'The woman looked as if she was going to have a fit but her husband arrived in their car just in time. She quickly walked over to it and shouted behind her really cockily: "You're only jealous because you can't afford one!" With that, the girl shouted out: "It takes 40 dumb animals to wear a fur coat but only one to wear it." The woman nearly choked. I had to go up to them and ask what it was all about. I finished up joining the same anti-fur group as them.'

The fur trade survives on just two things – greed and 'glamour'. All the other arguments put forward by those who trap and kill animals in the wild, or breed them in captivity, are nothing more than excuses.

Right across the world, most people are rejecting fur but the few who still insist on wearing dead animals are keeping the fur trade alive. Most governments turn their back on the suffering and say they have too many other important things to do. But some governments, such as those in the USA, Canada and Russia, actually support it.

It's difficult to be accurate about the number of animals killed but it ranges between 50 and 100 million. Of these, about 20 million are caught and killed in the wild. They're not killed because they're dangerous or a pest or for food, but only because they have beautiful fur coats. Think of almost any furry creature and someone is out to kill it – either legally or illegally.

The lynx and the fox, the sable and the squirrel, the wolf and the racoon are all hunted and killed, and about 16 other species as well, including the bear, badger, otter, beaver and, of course, mink. Once fur mostly came from the tropical regions of the world but having wiped out most of those animals it now tends to come from cold countries, where smaller animals are the target. Even in Britain some red foxes are trapped and killed for their fur.

Death trap

The most common method used for catching these beautiful wild creatures is the steel–jawed leghold trap. It consists of two hinged, spring–loaded, semicircular jaws which are forced apart until they form a flat circle and are held like that with a metal plate. The trap is then hidden beneath leaves, grasses or snow, and when an animal steps on the plate the jaws spring together with tremendous force, slamming shut on the animal's paw or leg. Often its bones will be broken, its blood vessels severed and its skin torn and ripped.

An official British inquiry into the leghold trap described it as 'a diabolical instrument which causes an incalculable amount of suffering'. As a result, they were banned in Britain and 65 other countries, but with appalling hypocrisy – the kind of cynical 'money first' attitude responsible for most world trade – it is still quite legal to import fur from animals caught by leghold traps.

The animal will remain in the trap, terrified and in great pain – and increasingly hungry and thirsty – for hours or even days, until the hunter returns to check it.

Some animals are so desperate to escape that they gnaw off their own paws. It happens so often that trappers even have a term for it – 'wring off'.

The hunter obviously isn't worried about the animal's suffering – in fact his only concern is not to damage the 'pelt' (the skin and its fur). Rarely does he shoot the animal because bullets cost money. He may club it to death but he is more likely to stand on it, one foot on the throat and one on the chest until the animal suffocates. That way no damage is done to the fur. Believe it or not but this is the method of killing recommended by the Californian State government.

Some animals such as beaver, mink and muskrat are caught in traps under water and held until they drown – something the fur trade still claims is humane. To any normal human being, drowning is quite clearly not humane but 'researchers' put it to the test. They captured some of these animals and put them in traps, held them below water and watched and counted while they drowned. It took most beavers as long as nine-and-a-half minutes to die while one's heart didn't stop beating for 25 minutes.

In my eyes, there is no difference between the trappers and researchers and I will never, ever understand how people can make a career out of inflicting pain and death. The cold, calculated, compassionless cruelty of the researchers is just as brutal as that of the trappers.

Other methods of trapping wild animals include the conibear trap and the snare. Theoretically, the conibear trap kills very quickly but only if all the circumstances are right – the right animal of the right size. Often it is the wrong animal and the wrong size and instead of springing shut

11

on the neck, the trap crushes the head or chest and the outcome is again a long, agonising wait for death.

The snare is a noose of wire which tightens around the animal's neck. The more it struggles in fear and panic, the tighter the noose gets until the animal is strangled.

None of these methods are fussy about who they kill. Any animal which stumbles into them will die and the result is a devastating assault on wildlife. The trappers dismiss these unwanted animals as 'trash'. On average, three trash animals die for every fur animal. So, to make a racoon fur coat will cost the lives of 40 racoons and 120 other animals.

All the people involved in killing animals, whoever they are and whatever the animal, always have a string of reasons to try to justify what they do. Almost always, these arguments seem to be nonsense – simply to justify their continued profits. The fur trade is no different to any other.

They say that trapping is a useful method of conservation – a way of managing wildlife. The opposite is true and wonderful creatures such as the margay, lynx, ocelot and Geoffroy's cat have been taken to the brink of extinction. The beaver and wolf are also perilously close to disappearing forever while for the snow leopard it is probably too late for survival – only about 500 remain. The sea mink has gone, trapped out of existence, and the same would have happened to the sea otter but trapping was stopped just in time to save it.

Most spotted cats throughout the world – including the leopard, cheetah and jaguar – have been so devastated by hunting that they are close to extinction. (See Chapter 12 for the lowdown on what has happened to tigers.) In fact most wild cats everywhere in the world are endangered thanks to the trappers.

Of course, attitudes have changed over the years and nowhere near so many animals are killed now as they were in the last century or just 20 or 30 years ago. In the early days of British rule in North America, by far the biggest and most profitable business was the Hudson Bay Company. Almost all its wealth came from trapping wild animals. Even in 1919, an unbelievable 107 million animals pelts from 125 different species were sold in the US. Whereas in 1999, 'only' 3.5 million animals were trapped for fur in the US.

This sales blurb from a 1960 advert by one of the world's most expensive fur-coat makers just about says it all: 'Max Bogen regret that [fur coat] No. 17 in our catalogue is no longer available. Unfortunately, a Himalayan snow leopard perfect enough to become a Max Bogen fur coat has not been sighted in over two years. But you may be sure that when the right one comes along, it'll end up at Max Bogen' (W Conway, 'Consumption of Wildlife by Man', *Animal Kingdom*, 2 June 1968).

Another excuse is that trapping is vital to the survival of indigenous native peoples. Again, this is nonsense. Native peoples account for just one animal in every four hundred that are trapped. Most trappers are amateurs who, unbelievably, do it for 'fun'. This is what one man wrote to a trapping magazine: 'It is just plain fun. Every set and every catch is a new adventure and a new surprise. That's fun!'

It's 'fun' watching a harmless animal writhing in agony with a broken leg and then beating it to death! There is something extremely frightening about such people and I don't believe that they could restrict this violence and contempt for life to non-human animals. It's why I believe that ending animal abuse is important for people as well.

Fur farming

The most common defence offered by people who insist on wearing fur coats is that the fur comes from 'ranch'-bred animals. Doesn't that sound wonderful? The claim is that animals bred to be killed for fur have a fine life and there's nothing to worry about in terms of animal welfare.

Mink and foxes are the animals most commonly bred for fur and their homes are far from being a ranch. In fact they are wire cages – row upon row of them. Mink are allowed just 60 cm by 37 cm, arctic foxes 112 cm by 70 cm. Both these animals would naturally travel miles in a single day and yet it is thought acceptable to take away their freedom and subject them to a pen little longer than their bodies.

Every year, 25 million mink and 3 million foxes live and die in these conditions. Those countries mainly responsible are Scandinavia, Russia and the USA. Denmark alone has 10,000 mink farms and kills over 9 million, while Finland is responsible for 2 million fox deaths.

What makes farming both these wild creatures particularly cruel is that they are naturally highly intelligent and inquisitive but they are very solitary. They have evolved to live on their own and defend their territories against all comers. In factory farms, not only can they barely move, they are forced into contact with thousands of their own kind which is extremely stressful. The result is that they often mutilate themselves or turn to cannibalism.

Maybe it's fortunate for them that their lives – or most

of them at any rate — are short. Breeding animals are mated in February, give birth in May, their young are weaned in six or seven weeks and killed in November at seven months old.

As you would probably expect, the dying is as brutal as the living. Mink are sometimes killed by injection, by having their necks broken or, the most common way, is to pile them all into a box that is connected to the exhaust pipe of a car or van engine. The engine is started and the exhaust fumes enter the box and kill the animals with carbon monoxide.

Over the years, many people have made comparisons between factory farming and the dreadful concentration camps of World War II. It is the same utter lack of compassion that allows both monstrosities to happen. So maybe it's not surprising that this exhaust method of killing mink was exactly the same method first used by the Nazis to kill Jews, gypsies, gays, disabled people and communists.

For foxes death is usually by electrocution, sometimes from a car battery. They are forcibly held so they can't move and an electrode is clamped in their mouth. Another electrode is forced into their rectum and the current switched on. No training or instruction of any kind is required before a person can carry out the slaughter.

As all these wild animals are being trapped into oblivion, experiments are going ahead to factory farm more animal species for fur.

Hell for leather

The one skin that most people wear without ever thinking about it is leather. The usual excuse is that it is just a small part of the meat trade and animals aren't killed for the leather, it's just a by-product.

Like all other businesses, animal farming survives because it makes money for those involved. Every part of the animal that is sold brings money to the industry and helps to keep it going. This includes: blood sold for fertilisers and pet food; hair for brushes and stuffing furniture; bone used for bone meal, another kind of fertiliser; hooves and horns are turned into gelatine, which finds its way into a whole range of foods including jellies, biscuits, many sweets, capsules for vitamins and even photographic film and match heads; and, of course, the skin, which is cured and tanned to make leather. Take away any of these and the profits start to disappear. When the whole trade becomes unprofitable, the killing stops.

Leather is made from the skins of pigs and sheep but most commonly is made from cattle. Like so many other things in life, cattle slaughtering has become very automated. As we will see in Chapter 8, after the cows enter the slaughterhouse they are shot through the head with a steel bolt to supposedly make them unconscious. In some cases it doesn't work at all and in others the cow recovers consciousness.

The cow is hauled up by one leg and its throat is cut where it joins the chest. It is the bleeding that actually kills the animal but the production line is so fast that when it moves on to the next stage, the skinning, the cow is sometimes still alive and still conscious. Its whole skin is automatically ripped off its body by a mechanical skinner before it reaches the next stage, where it is 'paunched' – its stomach cut open and its intestines removed.

It's not just countries such as the UK or USA that are cruel to cows. Surprisingly, one of the biggest leather producers in the world is India. While many people in India are Hindus and still hold cows as sacred, most look the other way as cows and buffaloes are killed for meat and leather. International shops routinely use skins from cows slaughtered in India.

The killing of cattle is legal in only a few Indian states, which means that cows are marched for hundreds of miles before reaching an abattoir. An investigation by People for the Ethical Treatment of Animals (PETA) revealed that animals are beaten mercilessly and driven forward in the searing heat. Their tails are deliberately broken and tobacco and chilli peppers are rubbed into their eyes to force them to stand up when they collapse. Their hooves are often bleeding and worn down to stumps.

When transported by lorry, cattle are so overcrowded that they are unable to avoid trampling, gouging and even suffocating one another. When they are unloaded, the cows who can still stand are pulled or forced to jump from the high lorry, often breaking legs and pelvises. Those who have collapsed are dragged from the trucks and left lying on the ground where the other cows are unloaded on top of them.

Many people who accept that farmed animals are killed for leather would be shocked to discover that their trainers or boots may be made not from a cow hide but from kangaroo (see Chapter 3), pony or even dog skin.

Pony skin is a by-product of killing horses for meat, a practice that goes on all over Europe including four abattoirs in Britain. Although the UK has banned the live export of horses, the rest of Europe still transports horses in appalling conditions. An investigation by the International League for the Protection of Horses revealed that 80,000 were taken from Russia and Eastern Europe to Italy in 1998. A lorry was followed which was carrying 23 animals. It was on the move for 47 hours and stopped for only five hours in total. When off-loaded, the horses were lame and highly stressed – one was dragged out dying. The others were killed in front of each other. Anyone who buys pony-skin items is supporting this trade.

Dog leather is sold worldwide and labelled as cow skin. More than 500 dogs are violently slaughtered every week in rural Thailand. The dogs are confined to crowded, filthy bamboo pens and routinely go days without being fed before being killed. Many of them are beaten to death or are sliced with a knife and tied upside down from trees and left to bleed. Similar reports come from India.

The luxury end of the leather market is equally brutal. Alligators and crocodiles are clubbed to death for their skins; ostriches are farmed and turned into shoes, wallets and handbags; and snakes such as the boa constrictor and cobra are skinned alive.

Whether cows, dogs, pigs or horses, the leather industry depends upon the deaths of millions of animals each year. It's fashion without compassion and should be given the boot!

Success Stories

- The number of people in Britain who wear a fur coat has dropped from 22 per cent in 1987 to just 7 per cent in 1996. And those who want a ban on the trapping of animals for fur has increased from 70 per cent in 1987 to a huge majority of 87 per cent in 1996. It's a similar story in the US – three quarters of the public want leghold traps banned and 63 per cent want the making of fur coats outlawed.

- The sale of fur in the UK dropped from £80 million worth of business in 1984 to less than £50 million by 1990. In the US, fur-industry profits have been cut by half since the mid-1980s, with Evans, the largest fur retailer, making losses of $12 million in 1999 ('Sandy Parker Reports', *International Fur News*, 29 November 1999).
- Most of the large stores in Britain have dropped their fur departments – even Harrods after selling fur for a century.
- Some of the best known swank designers in the world, such as Red or Dead, Eddie Bauer, Oleg Cassini and Norma Kamali are refusing to have their name associated with fur and many top models, such as Claudia Schiffer, won't wear it.
- In 1994, People for the Ethical Treatment of Animals (PETA) occupied Calvin Klein's office in New York; less than a month later he announced he would no longer design fur.
- Austria has closed all its 43 fur farms within 10 years of anti-fur campaigners launching an attack on the industry.
- After a two month campaign in 2000 by PETA, the international clothes chain The Gap stopped selling leather from India.

Action for Animals

- Don't wear fur!
- Don't buy leather! Do buy the animal-free leather-look alternatives. Look for shoes and other items that

are 'synthetic' or 'man-made' – they're in most high-street stores and usually cheaper than leather. For a free list of mail-order companies selling everything from shoes to jackets and belts contact Viva! in the UK, and in the USA, contact PETA.

- Speak out! Contact PETA – ask for their Fur is Dead and anti-leather action packs which include stickers, anti-fur cards to educate fur wearers, fact sheets and leaflets.
- Streak out! PETA run the 'I'd rather go naked than wear fur' campaign. Ask for details on how to hold a publicity stunt wearing nothing but a banner!
- Support the Coalition to Abolish the Fur Trade (CAFT) and the Respect for Animals campaigns for a ban on fur farming and to encourage retailers not to stock real fur.
- There are 13 mink farms in Britain producing 100,000 pelts a year. The Labour government has promised to close these farms by offering compensation to the farmers and banning any more mink farms from opening. Write to your MP (find out their name by calling 020 7219 3000) asking them to support the ban and the Prime Minister asking him to make sure Labour keeps their promise to ban mink farming. Contact them both at the House of Commons, London SW1A 0AA.
- Write to the Indian Embassy, urging them to help stop cruelty to India's cows:
  The High Commissioner
  Office of the High Commission for India
  Aldwych
  London WC2 4NA
- Write to the Ambassador of Thailand, urging him to use his influence to stop the hideous slaughter of dogs

for leather in his country:
The Ambassador of Thailand
The Royal Thai Embassy
29 Queen's Gate
London SW7 5JB

- Support the International League for the Protection of Horses (ILPH) campaign to end the live export of horses in Europe.

'I believe that to be truly glamorous you need dignity. Murdering innocent animals for fashion's sake has to be the most undignified of actions – cowardly and unnecesssary.'
Yasmin le Bon, top model

'Wearing fur is not morally acceptable and it's not stylish. I'd rather be on the dole than produce real-fur clothing for my collections.'
Wayne Hemingway, founder of fashion house Red or Dead

Chapter 2

Killing for Kicks

Hunting and Fighting Animals for Pleasure

Jasmine Carter is 16 and lives in Lancaster, a city not far from the Lake District. One day, on the spur of the moment, she and a friend got on a bus and went to visit this beautiful part of Britain.

'Things just seemed to be getting on top of me. I'd been having a row with my mum, my school work wasn't going that well and some divvy called Steve had been getting on my nerves. I just felt like I wanted to get away from it all for a few hours, to go somewhere beautiful that would make me think about other things.

'My friend Katie and I got on a bus early in the morning and went to Grasmere. My family used to go there quite a lot when I was a kid but I hadn't been back for two or three years. It didn't seem to have changed at all. There were the same beautiful stone houses, gorgeous little shops, trees and behind them all – mountains.

'There's a lovely little veggie café where you can sit outside overlooking a river and sparrows, chaffinches, robins and even pied wagtails come under your table to pick up crumbs. A female chaffinch was brave enough to take them right from the table top in front of us. By the time we'd finished our late breakfast, I'd already chilled out and my worries were almost forgotten.

'We walked through the town and out the other side, up a narrow road lined with stone walls and archways of trees which were all beginning to come into leaf. We walked along it chatting.

'When the road met a river and did a 90 degree turn, we left it and crossed a little bridge. We were then in open countryside and followed the bank of the river towards a mountain in the distance that seemed to shut off the end of the valley. A tumbling waterfall cascaded down its side but it was so far away it looked motionless. This was the life!

'Then I heard a sound that went right through me and I immediately recognised it as a hunting horn. My heart sank and my stomach churned. It was the first time I'd even heard one for real. But I couldn't see horses anywhere.

'On the right hand side of the valley I could see a pack of hounds tearing along through the bracken and rocks and I could just about catch the sound of their baying. They were so far away I could only just see them. They made a sudden turn, headed down into the valley bottom ahead of us and up the other side. But still I couldn't see any horses. I thought that they must be exercising the hounds and so I began to relax about it.

Again, just as quickly, the hounds changed direction and headed back down towards the river but this time they were heading more or less right for us. Then I saw something which I swear made my heart stand still. Just ahead of them was this streak of red and I realised it was a fox, running for its life.

'I don't know if it was a he or a she but it ran straight into the river about 25 yards ahead of us and lost its footing in the rocky stream. I had been watching the fox so closely I hadn't seen the hounds but one of them leaped into the water from the bank. It bit into the fox near its tail and, within a split second, the two of them were surrounded by most of the other hounds barking and yowling at the top of their voices. The fox completely disappeared under the mass of bodies. I could see the hounds pulling with all their might and shaking their heads like crazy.

'Katie and I had started running and had almost caught up to them. We were screaming and shouting. One by one the hounds started leaving the water but the fox was dead. One was carrying what looked like a leg, another a piece of flesh. All of them had bloody mouths.

'Only then did I see a group of older people leaning on a fence just a few yards away. While we were shaking with anger at the cruelty we'd witnessed, they were smiling and laughing and chatting away. I think they were mostly laughing at us.

'I couldn't tell you what I said to them even if I could remember because it was extremely rude. One old farmer threatened me with a big walking stick and told me to go back to the city – or words to that effect. We did, but not before Katie and I had both given him and the rest of them some more of our thoughts to take home.'

What Jasmine and Katie saw was probably the John Peel hunt – not the DJ(!), but the one made famous by the traditional song 'D'ye ken John Peel...'. They don't use horses because the valleys are too steep and rocky, so all the killing is done on foot. But, horses or not, it is just another form of legalised animal abuse – lasting two or three hours before exhaustion brings a painful and bloody end for the fox.

Hunting of all kinds takes place all over the world and has done for centuries. Despite claims that the instinct to kill lies deep within all of us, hunting has always been carried out by a minority of people.

The history of those obsessed with hunting, even the recent history, is a shameful one. When Europe's colonisers arrived in Africa for the first time, they didn't rub their eyes in disbelief at the wonders they saw. Almost their first action was to organise formal hunting parties to shoot wild animals in their millions, leaving most of them to rot where they fell. Meanwhile, they enslaved the people of the continent, transporting them across the world to work the plantations of America and the West Indies.

As recently as the 1950s, the Duke of Edinburgh was filmed sitting atop a splendidly attired elephant as he took part in a tiger shoot in India. He got his kill, shooting one of these beautiful creatures which is now facing extinction. This scene keeps coming back to haunt the man who is now President of the World Wildlife Fund and, like other members of the royal family, he still participates in organised shoots of birds such as pheasants (*Daily Express*, 8 August 1998).

Bye bye bison

The history of hunting in the US is just as dishonourable. The Great Plains of America were inhabited by over 60 million wonderful animals – the huge and beautiful bison. When they migrated, their hooves sounded like distant thunder and could be heard long before the herds came into sight.

Evolution had not equipped them to recognise the

crack of a rifle shot as dangerous so they would simply carry on grazing when someone fired. It was to be their downfall. So-called 'sportsmen' would line up and shoot them dead in countless numbers while the animals ignored them. With the coming of the railway, train loads of sportsmen would be ferried out into the prairies where the train would stop in the middle of a bison herd. The men didn't even bother to get out of the train. They lowered the windows and began their killing spree.

When the train eventually got up steam and headed back to the city, the prairie was left littered with thousands of dead and dying animals. Within 150 years, the bison had almost disappeared and by the late 1800s were thought to be extinct. It was only by chance, many years later, that a few scattered animals were discovered. From them, a few tens of thousands of bison have been bred and although they have avoided extinction, they no longer live their nomadic life. The prairies they once inhabited have been handed over to domestic cattle, who are now well advanced in destroying these unique pastures.

It was also in the US that the passenger pigeon existed. It would migrate the 3000 miles from the east coast to the west in countless millions – so many that the sky was said to go dark for hours as the flock passed over. It was men's idea of sport to stand beneath these huge flocks and blast the birds out of the sky. So successful were they at doing it that the passenger pigeon is now extinct.

You would think that with this history, American citizens would value the wildlife that remains but nothing could be further from the truth. For some people, the right to hunt and to own rifles and shotguns is considered an essential part of American life. It has become a highly political issue. As a result, the continuing assault on the continent's wildlife is tremendous.

There is nothing pleasant about this brutal, redneck, macho approach to the slaughter of wild animals although the ritual and cut-glass accents of hunters involved in British fox hunting are no better. The latter has traditionally been the sport of the aristocracy and this is why it has managed to survive for so long. It's so much a part of the ruling class that hunting terms are even used in the UK's Houses of Parliament. The politicians who are responsible for seeing that MPs vote the way their political party wants them to, are called 'whips' – a term taken directly from hunt 'whippers in', who keep the hounds in order. (Actually, you're not supposed to call them dogs, they are hounds.)

Hunting is an extremely expensive pastime. Those who 'ride to hounds' have to buy very costly horses, tack and clothing. They have to stable and feed the horses all year round, transport them to the place of hunting and pay expensive fees for belonging to the hunt. This money pays for the kennels, the upkeep of the hounds and the salaries of full-time kennel workers and huntsmen.

About 20,000 foxes are killed every year by about 350 hunts. Each hunt includes the hunt master, a huntsman (paid employee), whippers in and about 30 hunt followers on horseback, 40 hounds and several 'terriermen' in four-wheel drive vehicles. Other people follow the hunt on foot or by car.

The class division that existed when hunting first started can still be seen. At the top of the heap are the masters, wealthy and usually land owners. At the bottom are the terriermen, the working-class labourers who carry out the hunts' really dirty work.

The 'sports' that these men traditionally followed – cock fighting, badger baiting, bull and bear baiting and dog fighting – have all been outlawed as cruel. However, the power and influence of their masters has ensured that their 'sport' has continued. If all this sounds to you like something from another century, you're right, that's exactly what it is.

Fox facts

The reason why fox hunting is such an important issue is because it's a classic example of how power and influence can pervert truth and honesty. But many of its problems also apply to other forms of hunting. Let's get one thing absolutely straight – the reason people hunt is because they find it entertaining. Any reasons they give such as controlling pests or protecting livestock are just excuses. If you look at hunting objectively, not even one of its claims stand up to investigation.

Fox hunting started in Britain about 250 years ago when all the wild boar and wolves had been hunted to extinction and deer had been reduced to a few herds, mostly on big estates. Before that, foxes had been completely ignored.

Foxes are a small wild dog that have shown themselves to be amazingly adaptable and are now almost as much a part of towns as they are the countryside. Like all dogs, they are both hunters and scavengers. But foxes are not fighters – they will back away from any kind of confrontation rather than get into a fight. Video footage shows that when a fox and cat bump into each other, which they do frequently, it's the fox that gives the cat a wide berth.

Hunting takes place all over Europe and in parts of the US but its natural home is Britain. Here, it takes place between the beginning of November and April. As female foxes – vixens – give birth to their cubs in March, it means they are hunted when they are pregnant or nursing their cubs. The cubs of any vixen who is killed during this time will starve to death.

The main diet of foxes is rabbits, rats, voles, earthworms and carrion (anything that's already dead). They largely feed at night and lie low during the day. Their 'earth' – usually a hole in the ground – is used as a home to give birth to and protect the cubs. Once weaned, they spend the majority of their time above ground, except in emergencies.

Terror men

The hunt identifies particular areas that have foxes – usually coverts, small areas of woodland. The terriermen start work before the hunt and scour the area for fox earths, which they block up. It is illegal for them to block badger setts but they often do this too. It's perhaps not surprising that almost every man ever found guilty of badger baiting – setting dogs onto a badger who cannot escape – has been a hunt terrierman.

The following day the hounds are sent into one of the coverts and if they 'put up' a fox, the chase is on. It can last for hours until the fox either escapes or is caught and torn to pieces. If the fox finds an earth, or sometimes even a badger sett, which hasn't been blocked up, it may take refuge inside. But, sadly, it offers no escape.

The terriermen arrive and their first task is to put a small terrier dog down the entrance of the earth in the hope of driving the fox out. The terrier will attack the fox and may stay underground biting and tearing at what bits of the fox it can get hold of while the terriermen begin to dig the animals out. Fox earths can be deep and the process can take hours.

I have seen one piece of video footage which makes me both sad and angry every time I think of it. It shows the end of a dig out which has taken nearly three hours. During the whole of this time the fox will have been frightened and highly stressed. The footage shows a terrierman holding up the screaming vixen by the scruff of her neck and he is laughing. She is so terrified that she urinates and defecates while she is held in the air. You can clearly see her swollen teats that are seeping milk, which means that somewhere she has young cubs waiting to be fed. Again the terrierman finds this amusing and points to them.

Finally, bored with having his picture taken, he puts the vixen on the ground, stands on her with one foot and then beats her to death with a shovel. Throughout this whole process he never stops laughing or smiling. That man is probably out there now, part of someone's community – a man utterly devoid of compassion, who finds humour in terror and suffering.

Reasons to kill

Of course, those involved in hunting try to hide the cruelty with strict social rules about hunt 'etiquette' (manners) and dress. They like to pretend that they are the only ones who know anything about the countryside and are a part of rural tradition. They may be part of recent tradition but they obviously know nothing about wild animals because their excuses in support of hunting are nonsense.

They say that if foxes weren't hunted they would over-run the countryside. There are about 350,000 foxes in Britain and almost all of them are killed every year – by cars, by shooting, gassing and snaring, and some by hunting, but only a small minority. It is an amazing onslaught on one species, which survives only because it still manages to have cubs.

Even if no foxes were killed, they still wouldn't take over because they are superb at controlling their own numbers according to availability of food. If food is scarce the less dominant vixens stop coming into season. Foxes form family groups that defend their own territory against intruding foxes, and this helps maintain stability of numbers in each area. The fox population would not explode if all methods of fox killing were stopped and this was demonstrated by Aberdeen University in a three-year study.

The other claim made in support of hunting is that foxes destroy livestock, particularly sheep and hens. For a start, almost all hens are kept inside huge industrial sheds and never see a fox. On free-range farms, foxes can be successfully kept out with electric fences and by ensuring all the hens are securely inside when the light begins to fade.

As for sheep, there have been three studies into fox predation on lambs in Britain – by the Government, Bristol University and the hunters' magazine *The Field*. The Government said that the problem was 'insignificant'. Bristol University said that far from being a problem, the effect of the fox on the countryside was beneficial. Even the hunters' favourite publication could only come up with a figure of one lamb per hundred being taken by foxes. It compares with 20 lambs per hundred that die because of cold, hunger and neglect by the farmer. The chances are that the lambs that were taken by foxes were likely to be those that were sickly and dying.

As one farmer told me, no mother sheep is ever going to allow a fox to grab her lamb and the fox won't risk confrontation with an angry ewe. Of course, now that ewes are being forced to have three lambs, it might be difficult for her to protect all of them – but whose fault is that?

The usual insult hurled at foxes is that they're vicious and if they get in a henshed will kill all the hens for fun and take only one to eat. The only animal that kills in large numbers for fun is us – humans.

In nature, a fox is never surrounded by flapping, frightened birds because they would simply be able to fly away. Its instincts are to kill when it has the chance and only humans can present it with such an opportunity when they artificially confine birds in a shed. Researchers have witnessed this killing frenzy in other carnivorous animals including sharks. It's nothing more than instinct.

If hunting was about controlling fox populations, fast running dogs such as greyhounds or lurchers would be used and the whole thing would be over in seconds – but they aren't. In fact, the hounds are specially bred to run more slowly than the fox and to sustain a prolonged chase. The fox outruns the hounds until it is exhausted and the bigger and stronger hounds are then able to catch it. The longer the fox can keep up its efforts, the more so-called 'sport' is obtained; therefore a weak, elderly or pregnant fox provides only a short hunt. A young, fit and strong fox can last up to two hours before it succumbs to fatigue, but the hounds can run for six or seven hours if necessary. Foxes are not naturally adapted to endure long periods of pursuit and must suffer great distress.

Baby butchery

One aspect of fox hunting rarely mentioned is 'cubbing' which is used to train the foxhounds. Because the hounds have no natural instinct to kill foxes, they have to be trained by being taken out from August to October with older dogs and set onto young fox cubs. A small wood is surrounded by hunters on horseback and on foot, and the hounds are sent in to attack the cubs. If a young fox tries to escape, the hunters slap their saddles and shout to terrify the animal back to the hounds. Clifford Pellow, a professional huntsman for 20 years, declared: 'Cub hunting is a barbaric, hideous business in which the victims are still completely and utterly inexperienced and dependent on their mothers' (LACS, 'Hunting', 1997). Ten thousand cubs are killed this way each year.

And what about the hounds? At six years old (half their life expectancy) they are shot, to be replaced by younger hounds.

Love a duck?

All kinds of hunting used to take place for fun, including shooting songbirds such as thrushes and skylarks. In some countries it is still quite legal to shoot songbirds and they have been illegally trapped in Britain and sold to Malta to satisfy the huntsmen's bloodlust.

Try to work out the logic in this. In the mid 1900s laws were introduced to protect some birds from being hunted in Britain. They included most of the birds you see regularly in your garden – linnets, finches, tits, blackbirds, wrens, robins and so on. Missed off the list were birds such as ducks, geese, pheasants, partridge, grouse and woodcock. They are just as beautiful as the protected birds, equally harmless and they make a wonderful contribution to the countryside.

The reason they were not protected was that lords and ladies and wealthy people loved to shoot these birds and have them served to eat at their dining table. Preservation again took second place to political influence – and still does. Can you think of one good reason why a harmless little creature like the duck should be killed – or a magnificent bird like the Canada goose, who migrates to Europe all the way from Siberia? I certainly can't.

The reason I mention this is to show that the killers and animal abusers are still protected – it is officially considered people's right to shoot and injure just for fun. There are always reasons to justify it but, like those for fox hunting, they never stand up to investigation.

Otter misery

Take the otter. This glorious little animal used to be common in British rivers and, just as with the fox, men (and some women) with packs of dogs would hunt it. Their excuse was that they were protecting fish stocks, conveniently forgetting that otters feed mostly on eels.

The end to the hunt was as brutal as any. When the otter had been cornered, exhausted, confused and frightened, one of the hunt would hold a long pole, forked at the end, over the back of the otter's neck. The otter was then forced underwater and held there until it drowned.

These 'heroes' would then lift its little dead body aloft and go off to celebrate their 'bravery'.

The huntsmen's right to hunt the otter was fought for until the bitter end. Even when the otter was on the point of extinction in the UK, they still argued their right to go on killing!

Another glorious animal is still hunted with dogs – the hare. As modern intensive agriculture destroys Europe's pasture lands, so the hare loses its home and is rapidly disappearing. But it hasn't stopped people from hunting it. Some are even used for a sport called 'hare coursing', where two dogs chase it together. The dog who can make it turn the most number of times wins the course. Sometimes the hare escapes but frequently it is caught by one of the dogs and torn to pieces.

Deer and mink are also hunted with dogs. The sight of an exhausted deer collapsing in a river, with a huntsman throwing his full weight onto its horns in an attempt to force its head underwater to drown it says a lot about the cruelty of hunting. A magnificent stag, caught in a brick-yard with no escape, being torn at by a pack of dogs, watched by men and women dressed up in hunting finery and showing no remorse for their brutality, is a hard reality to understand.

States of death

Almost every country in the world indulges in hunting of one kind or another. But the one in which it has cleverly been associated with 'rights of the individual', 'liberty' and 'freedom' is the USA. It is none of these things for the animals that are slaughtered. It is, the hunters claim, a 'tradition' – a tradition of killing, crippling, extinction and ecological destruction. Hunters with rifles, shotguns, muzzleloaders, handguns and bows and arrows kill more than 200 million animals yearly, injuring and orphaning millions more.

The death toll is quite staggering as the US group The Fund for Animals has documented. They state that over 42 million mourning doves, 30 million squirrels, 28 million quail, 25 million rabbits, 20 million pheasants, 14 million ducks, 6 million deer and thousands of geese, bears, moose, elk, antelope, swans, cougars, turkeys, wolves, foxes, coyotes, bobcats, boars and other creatures are hunted annually in the US.

As usual, controlling numbers or saving animals from slow death by starvation are the most common excuses given. Most of the species killed are not overpopulated at all. Birds such as ring-necked pheasants are raised in pens and hand-fed before being released into the wild just before the hunting season. They are not native to the US and those that aren't shot, die from exposure or starvation.

Another excuse is that hunting is a method of managing wildlife, which is why wildlife agencies in most states work with hunters. But state wildlife agencies also make money out of hunters, providing them with animals to kill in return. They build roads through wild areas so hunters can gain access, they support hunting with protective laws, they educate hunters to make them more efficient killers and they fell forests and burn under-growth to provide food for 'game' such as deer. Other wildlife suffers in the process.

Many agencies are quite open about their role. Take Arizona, who state they are trying to provide more 'targets', such as pronghorn antelope, cottontail rabbits, quail and bighorn sheep. They say they want to provide 'recreational opportunity to as many individuals as possible' by improving access to the animals' habitat (Arizona Game and Fish Department, 'Strategic Plans for the Management of Arizona Game Species', 1992–1996).

Perhaps the most worrying claim of all from hunters is that they never kill threatened or endangered species. The truth is that they have helped to wipe out dozens of species, including the passenger pigeon as we have seen, the great auk and heath hen. They have taken many others, including the bison and the grizzly bear, to the brink of extinction. Even the US Government acknowledged this in 1973 when it said that: 'The two major causes of extinction are hunting and destruction of natural habitat.'

The threat is still real. Either wilfully or because they don't bother to identify their 'targets' properly, hunters continue to kill threatened and endangered species every year. They include such wonderful creatures as the gray wolf, bald eagle, grizzly bear and even critically endangered animals such as the Florida panther.

Perhaps the most sickening aspect is that for some animals even their breeding season isn't safe. While some agencies set hunting seasons for bears, squirrels and mountain lions, others don't. The babies of any mother killed by a 'sport' hunter are certain to die of starvation or predation.

Perhaps the greatest success of shooters is their use of the word 'sport'. It somehow gives the impression that the killing is fair and the animals stand a chance. The truth is that hunters go to great lengths to ensure that the animals stand no chance whatsoever.

Captured wild animals such as prairie dogs and pigeons are used in shooting contests. They are released in front of cheering crowds and shooters compete for money and prizes to see who can kill the most.

Gentle mourning doves pose no threat to anyone and yet they are lured to sunflower fields in what are called 'wing shoots' and are blasted out of the sky just for target practice. More than 20 per cent are injured and left to die where they fall.

Those bizarre people who want to put an animal's head on their wall often bait open land with piles of rotten food to attract bears or deer. The unwitting animals are shot at point-blank range while they feed.

Dogs with radio transmitters on their collars are used in 'hounding'. The dogs chase bears, cougars, racoons, foxes, bobcats and lynx, who seek refuge by climbing trees. The dogs remain on guard below. The killers then follow the radio signal and shoot the trapped animals out of the trees.

One of the corniest old claims made by hunters is that it is 'natural' for humans to hunt and we are driven by basic instincts. Oh yes? In the US, only five per cent of the population feel the need to kill wild animals and the number gets less every year. Unbelievably, the US Fish and Wildlife Service and most State wildlife agencies now sponsor youth recruitment hunts to try to keep the numbers up (The Fund for Animals, 'Your Government in Action: Teaching Children to Kill', 9 May 2000).

It seems far more natural for people to appreciate the countryside and wildlife rather than to destroy it, which is why 40 per cent of Americans are involved in bird-watching, wildlife photography, hiking and camping.

A load of bull

Hunting is not the only bloodsport done for fun. Bullfighting is one of the biggest rituals in Spain, France and Mexico which involves the death of thousands of animals every year.

The idea behind bullfighting – the one that its followers would like you to believe – is that it is a courageous, honourable ritual with one person's bravery pitted against a vicious and cunning animal. It is nothing like that. They do everything they can to stack the odds in favour of the 'matador' – the bullfighter.

The first thing that can happen is that the tips of the bull's horns are cut off. This ensures that the animal can't quite judge distances properly and he stands a good chance of missing the matador when he tries to gore him with his horns.

Before a fight, a bull is sometimes kept without water – even for days – until he is dying from thirst. Just before the fight he is given a huge bowl of wine to drink from. This ensures that he is literally drunk when he enters the ring and all his reactions are affected.

Another way of weakening the bull is to hold him captive in one of the passageways leading to the ring and then continuously drop heavy, sand-filled sacks onto his back. Another awful trick is to smear Vaseline over the bull's eyes so that his vision is badly blurred.

Now you would think that all that would be enough to ensure the bull offered no great threat to the matador. But that isn't the end of it. Once he enters the ring, he is goaded and teased by the 'picador' who rides a horse cloaked in a long skirt that comes almost to the ground. In his hand he carries a long, thick lance with a sharply pointed steel tip. The bull charges the picador and his horse and the picador aims his lance at the bull's neck muscles. Up to four thrusts will be given, leaving the animal in agony and weakening him still further.

He will often let the bull charge into the horse, the long skirt hiding where its horns tear into the soft under-belly of the terrified animal. I have been told that, some-times, the horse's vocal cords are severed so that the cheering crowds do not hear it whinnying in terror as it is gored in the stomach.

In the next stage of the fight, the 'banderilleros' take the stage holding decorated wooden stakes in their hand, each about half-a-metre long. Fixed to the end of each is a vicious steel spike about 20 cm long with a sharp hook on the end. They tease and taunt the bull and thrust these spikes deep into his back, in or near the wounds made by the picador.

Each time it happens the bull kicks and throws himself about in pain. Before long, a collection of these barbs are hanging from between his shoulder blades and he is covered with blood. Sadly, that also isn't the end. It is now the matador's turn.

The bull is now exhausted, confused and dying from blood loss and yet the matador is cheered like some kind of hero. His aim is to get as close to the bull's horns as he can without being gored and to 'turn' him – fool the creature into turning in the wrong direction. The mata-dor makes several passes with a red cape (it is red to hide bloodstains, not to attract the bull as he is colour-blind). When he has done this for long enough to show what a 'brave' person he is, the matador gets ready for the kill.

He takes a sword and conceals it in his cloak and

performs a few more turns. When the bull is totally worn out, simply standing there panting, the barbs still hanging from his flesh and his sides red with blood, the matador produces the sword, aims it at the bull's back and runs at him, thrusting the sword between the animal's shoulder blades and into his heart. At least that is the aim.

The sword may bounce off the spine or ribs and come out through the side of the bull. Or it may hit bone and fail to penetrate deeply. Sometimes it will pierce a lung and the bull will cough up great cascades of blood as he stands there, incapable any longer of defending himself.

Eventually the bull sinks slowly to the ground and collapses. If the matador is thought to have fought well he will be allowed to cut off the bull's ears or cut out his tongue. The bull may well be conscious when he does this.

I have seen a bull who had been pierced with a sword several times but still refused to collapse. The whole sorry spectacle finished up with the banderilleros swarming all over him, each one stabbing repeatedly with a dagger, hoping to cut through an artery.

When the bull has finally collapsed, he is dragged off by a team of mules to the slaughterhouse, which is a part of the bullring.

Meat from the bull is sold in local restaurants at a very high price simply because it was a 'fighting bull'. It is very rare that a bull survives or is allowed to live after a Spanish bullfight.

Success Stories

- In the UK three quarters of the population think hunting with dogs should be banned.

- The League Against Cruel Sports in Britain has 36 wildlife sanctuaries where no animal can be hunted and has persuaded landowners to ban hunting on over 200,000 hectares of land.
- Deerhunting with hounds is illegal in Scotland.
- Badger baiting in Britain was outlawed in the 1970s and the sett itself given protection in 1991.
- Over 150 UK local councils and 40 county wildlife trusts have banned hunting on their land, as has the Wildfowl and Wetland Trust, stopping some of Britain's biggest hunts.
- In the 1980s in the US, The Fund for Animals blocked the Federal Government and State of Minnesota from hunting or trapping wolves.
- In the 1990s, after casting a national spotlight on the hunting of bison who wander from Yellowstone National Park, The Fund for Animals pressured the state of Montana into banning it. The group also successfully used lawsuits to halt grizzly-bear hunting in Montana and a massive elk hunt in Arizona's Coconino National Forest.
- Over the past 10 years, the World Society for the Protection of Animals (WSPA) and other groups have prevented Spanish companies from starting bullfighting in Egypt, Mozambique, Russia, Poland, Hungary, Italy and Greece.
- Campaigners have changed the law in Bolivia, Panama, the Dominican Republic and the Canary Islands to stop bulls being stabbed or killed in bullfights.

Action for Animals

- Start scribbling! Some hunts still take place on public land. Find out if your local council still permits it and write to them.
- Most people want hunting banned. The Labour Government promised that they would do so and most of their politicians want it outlawed. It is an important time to write to your MP and the Prime Minister. You can find your MP's name by calling 020 7219 3000 and write to them both at the House of Commons, London SW1A 0AA.

Your name
Your address

Your MP's name (eg Iva Ban MP)
House of Commons
London SW1A 0AA

Dear MP's name

Masquerading behind the front of 'tradition', fox hunting is simply organised cruelty. Foxhounds are bred for a lengthy chase, rather than a quick kill. Young cubs and pregnant vixens are amongst the hunted victims. And all this for no reason – the fox population does not need 'controlling' and hunting makes no difference to overall fox numbers.

All hunting with dogs is inexcusable. Please work to ban it before the next general election.

Yours sincerely
Your name

- Write to the 'Letters Page' of your local newspaper – it's read by thousands of people.
- Contact a group such as the League Against Cruel Sports or the National Anti-Hunt Campaign and help them ban hunting.
- Don't go to a bullfight.
- Don't buy any bullfight souvenirs – bullfighting posters or postcards, toy bulls etc.
- Protest about bullfighting to your MEP (Member of European Parliament) – get the name and address by calling 020 7222 0411.
- Write to:
  The Ambassador of Spain
  Spanish Embassy
  39 Chesham Place
  London SW1 8QA
- Support the WSPA's campaign to end bullfighting. Contact them for free information.
- Fight Against Animal Cruelty in Europe (FAACE) work to end bullfighting and Spanish blood fiestas and have saved some of the victims. They need your help.

'Did you know that red deer are Britain's largest wild animals? How sickening that they are killed so cruelly in the name of "sport".'
Bill Oddie, TV presenter and ornithologist

'The desperate plight of these frightened, defenceless creatures makes me so very angry – we must all help to stop fox hunting.'
Sue Cook, TV presenter

Chapter 3

Under Fire

Hunting Animals for Profit

When you've been brought up to believe that certain things are normal and acceptable – because that's the way they've always been – it can take a strong personality to reject them. But that's exactly what Peter Pirelli, 14, did.

'I don't remember when I first started music lessons, I just know it was a long time ago. I also know that I didn't like them very much and Mum always had to nag me to go. If I'd had my way I would have given it up right at the start. But now that I'm quite good I really enjoy it.

'There was something my music teacher said when she was trying to be funny – about me "tinkling on the ivories". I didn't have a clue what she was on about but didn't want to look stupid. When I got home I asked my dad what she'd meant and he said that piano keys used to be made out of ivory.

'I wasn't sure if I'd understood him so I asked if he meant ivory as in elephants' tusks – and he said yes. He reckoned they were all made from plastic now and had been for years and years.

'The piano that I used at home was really, really old – an upright covered in fancy woodwork with candlestick holders on hinges. The white keys were a bit cracked in places and they weren't really white, more a dirty sort of yellow colour. They certainly didn't look like plastic to me. I asked him if he thought they were made out of ivory and he said "yes, probably", just like that.

'I couldn't believe it. I'd just been reading about elephants in Africa and India being killed in terrible ways for their tusks and here I was running my fingers over ivory piano keys made from dead elephants. It was disgusting.

'I told my dad I was never going to touch them again and he got really mad. Suddenly, I got this lecture about how animals have always been used for the benefit of humans and there was nothing wrong with that, it was just the natural way of things.

'In the end I had to agree that it wasn't sensible not to use my piano – it was probably about a zillion years old and it would make no difference to the elephant that had been killed for it. I didn't really accept this but I knew we couldn't afford another piano and I didn't want to make life difficult for everyone.

'But I said I would only use it if we joined a group that was fighting to save elephants – that way I reckoned we could make it up to the one whose ivory was in the front room. My dad really "went into one" but I wouldn't back down and I meant it. In the end my mum stepped in and worked out some sort of deal that kept the peace but meant we did join a group.

'When all these leaflets started to arrive about how elephants had nearly been wiped out in some places and how they were killed in really cruel ways, I made sure my dad saw every one of them. If I thought he hadn't read them I'd tell him every detail. I'm getting membership of another group fighting to save whales and dolphins as part of my next birthday present and no one even wants to argue about it. I think I've got through to them.'

Sometimes I find it amazing that young people like Peter think much more deeply about animals and the environment than their parents. You'd think that age would bring wisdom, but it doesn't always seem to work that way. And, of course, there's nothing worse than having your opinions dismissed because 'you're too young' – that's like saying that you won't mind animal abuse when you get older.

Throughout recent history, some animals have always been hunted and treated like they were coal, oil or wood – just another commodity to be exploited. Their feelings, their ability to suffer and their right to life have been completely ignored. It's usually about money but few people know just what a huge industry it used to be and still is in some countries.

In the seventeenth and eighteenth centuries, Europe's industries depended almost entirely on one animal. There was no petroleum oil from the ground then but all the pieces of machinery in the new industries (which were opening up everywhere during the industrial revolution) had to be lubricated so that they ran smoothly. It was the whale that was killed in massive numbers to achieve this.

Save the whale

Whale oil found its way into soap, margarine, cosmetics – almost anything that required fat or oil. Even its bones were used to make the corsets that gave women that uncomfortable and unnatural hourglass shape.

Before that, there had been so many whales in the oceans that old sailing ships used to keep a special watch in the bow of the ship to make sure they didn't run into them. It seems incredible that most whale species are now fighting for survival.

The scale of the oceans is almost breathtaking – they have an average depth of 400 metres and cover 75 per cent of the planet's surface. It is a huge volume of water, so no wonder it produced the biggest living creatures the world has ever seen.

There are two types of whale – 'baleen' and toothed. The blue whale is the biggest of all the whales, weighing as much as 120 tonnes, the equivalent to 2000 people or 30 elephants, and yet the biggest thing it eats is the size of a very small shrimp. It strains them through baleen – thin strips of a fringed, bone-like substance.

The sperm whale is a toothed whale and has the largest brain on earth. It can dive to a depth of 230 metres in search of its favourite food – giant squid. There are many different types of whale, dolphin and porpoise and all have been hunted at some time or other.

The slaughter of whales started as far back as the twelfth century and, as the years went by, the kill rate increased. To begin with the main target was the right whale, so called because it had a high oil content and was gentle, slow and easy to catch. It was the 'right' whale to kill. But the whalers did what hunters have always done – when they have almost wiped out one species, they move on to another. The right whale is now on the verge of extinction with only a few hundred remaining.

The sperm whale was another highly prized catch and for what? For its phlegm! It secretes a waxy substance called ambergris, seen as a 'vital' ingredient in perfume. Whales were killed in vast numbers so that women could douse themselves with an artificial smell!

The sperm whale was not easy to catch but its strong urge to protect its family was its downfall. If one family member was injured by harpoons, others would come to its aid, desperately trying to keep it afloat so it could breathe. They then became an easy target for the whalers.

Although a baby whale wasn't of much value, the whalers would target it, knowing that once they had injured it, its mother would come to its assistance and they could then kill her – the real target.

In the early days, whales were killed with hand harpoons – long poles with a barbed metal spike on the end which was driven into the animal's flesh. It might take 20 of these crude spears before the whale would lose its strength and start its long agonising death on the surface.

Then came the explosive harpoon, fired from a gun in the bow of the whaling ship. As the harpoon thuds into the whale's body, a grenade explodes, blasting a hole in the animal, causing enormous damage. But still it may be left to thrash around for hours in terrible pain before it finally dies. These days it is finished off with rifle fire or electric shocks, but these are neither quick, nor very effective and themselves cause great pain. There is no humane way of killing a whale.

The world's biggest whalers were the Americans and in the nineteenth century they had fleets all around the world. In the early 1900s, steam-powered ships that could go anywhere at any time began to increase the kill rate and the number of whales slaughtered each year rose from 10,000 in 1910 to 66,000 in 1961.

In 1986, after years of campaigning by millions of people, whaling came to an end – mostly. For some species this was probably too late because their numbers were too few to survive. For others and the many different types of dolphin, there is still a struggle for survival.

Some countries have started to fish for krill, the tiny shrimp-like creatures that provide much of the food for baleen whales. Starvation may be the result.

Overfishing in all the world's oceans has reduced food supplies for toothed whales and dolphins and many die when they become entangled in nets. Pollution from industry and ships also affects whales badly.

Whales are highly intelligent creatures and have a very strong sense of family, usually living together in small family groups known as 'pods'. They communicate with each other by what we have come to call 'songs' which can travel for up to 80 km through the water. These songs can have a haunting quality almost like cries, but they are incredibly complicated – far more than the sounds that make up human speech. We understand almost nothing about them.

In the face of all that's known about these wonderful creatures and their struggle for survival, three countries still insist on killing them. Norway and Japan, two of the wealthiest countries in the world, hunt minke whale. They claim it is for 'scientific' reasons to research how whale numbers are recovering. This is quite clearly a lie but these countries are determined to keep on whaling simply because it is part of their 'culture'.

The third place is just 200 miles off the coast of Scotland in the small islands called the Faroes, where one of the worst slaughter of whales happens every year. The way some people behave, you would think it was a party or national celebration as they flock down to the beaches to watch it.

Pilot whales pass the islands during their annual migration but between 500 and 3000 never complete their journey. They are driven into a bay by men in boats and to try to escape the whales swim further and further towards the shore. Eventually, they are driven into the shallow water by the beaches where other men are waiting with spears, knives and axes. They hack the pilot whales to death and the waters of the bay turn blood red and are thrashed into a scarlet foam by the dying animals.

Again you hear the same old cry from the Faroes' Government – that it is 'traditional' and necessary for food. Like the Norwegians and Japanese, the Faroese are wealthy people and can buy all the food they need by walking into a shop. There is absolutely no need to slaughter these amazing animals.

Bear facts

Perhaps one of the most disgusting and cruel hunts is for the moon bear in China. When caught they are kept in flat, rusty iron cages no bigger than the animal itself. There are 7500 caged bears throughout China and Korea. It's exactly as if they are in barred metal coffins but above ground. They can barely move at all and they live like that for years.

They all have an ugly wound in their side, often diseased and festering, from which a tube protrudes. It is connected directly to one of their internal organs – the gall bladder. Every so often, bile liquid from the gall bladder is extracted and the bears scream in agony as it happens. Bear bile is an ingredient in traditional Chinese medicine and is still used despite the fact that herbs and synthetic substances are known to cure the same illnesses. Bears are still hunted but, as there are only 20,000 remaining in the wild in all of China, most are now reared in captivity.

Elephants under threat

The elephant's huge ivory tusks, which can weigh nearly 200 kg, are a form of teeth. The elephants use them for defence and for moving obstacles. Ivory is known as 'white gold' and for centuries has been used for many things, but mostly just for decoration – usually carved trinkets, ornaments and jewellery. Not only was it used for Peter's piano keys, it was carved into every imaginable shape and form, including model elephants. This sums up the stupidity of the human race – they are prepared to buy a model of an animal they obviously admire and in so doing guarantee its destruction.

Although the slaughter had gone on for centuries, in both Africa and Asia where two different types of elephant live, it reached its peak comparatively recently. In the 10 years between 1978 and 1988, 700,000 African elephants were killed and their population crashed by more than half. Most of the slaughter was caused by poachers who killed the animals illegally. African elephants live south of the Sahara and were wiped out across the continent. Poaching was particularly high in Kenya, Zambia and Tanzania in the 1980s and Zimbabwe and South Africa produced ivory and leather from elephants for export.

A lot of money can be made from ivory, so in a country where many people are very poor, the temptation is great. Although it is the Africans who mostly do the killing, it is the people in the wealthy West and Far East (particularly Japan) who buy the ivory who perpetuate the killing.

Because guns and bullets cost money, the poachers often use other, cheaper methods to catch these huge animals. The favourite one is the snare, a wire loop that tightens around the elephant's foot or leg.

Having set the snare, it might be weeks before the poacher returns to check it. During this time, a trapped elephant will slowly starve to death. Unable to escape, the thin wire loop cuts deeper and deeper into its flesh. It has been known for a snare to cut right through an elephant's foot.

Another method is the poisoned dart. The particular poison used guarantees a slow and lingering death for the elephant as parts of its body slowly rot away, until it finally collapses from pain and weakness. This can take weeks, and while the elephant struggles to survive it is followed at a distance by the poachers, watching and waiting their chance to cut out the creature's tusks. They rarely bother to kill the elephants before digging out the tusks by the roots.

We tend to think that all these mass animal killings are in the past and we've learnt by our mistakes. If only! A few years ago in the US, it was considered great sport and very profitable to hunt wild horses. They were sometimes shot from helicopters and their carcasses sold for use in canned food for cats and dogs. The biggest wildlife massacre on land that has ever taken place is happening right now and getting worse year by year. It is the kangaroo kill in Australia.

Kangaroo kill

The kangaroo is a unique animal in that the mother gives birth to her baby when it is little more than an embryo, no bigger than your fingernail. He quickly makes his way across her fur and into the pouch of loose flesh on the front of her stomach, where there are teats, and it is here that the tiny little 'joey' remains until he has grown enough to face the outside world. Even when he's quite big, he will often scoot back to Mum's pouch if he's frightened. Fortunately, the skin stretches like elastic to accommodate these sometimes not-so-little creatures.

There are many different kinds of kangaroo and wallaby but they all raise their young in this way. They are called 'marsupials' and live in large family groups of up to 80 called 'mobs'.

Australia's record on wildlife is an appalling one. Since the white settlers first arrived there about 200 years ago, they have exterminated more species of animals than on any other continent – and that includes six species of kangaroo. But that hasn't stopped them from continuing the kill.

As you'll have gathered by now, the secret to operating a massacre of innocent animals is to provide excuses to keep people quiet. Most never check the claims, they just repeat them and say things like: 'Well, it has to be done, doesn't it?' That's precisely what's happened with kangaroos.

The reason why kangaroos are such strange and wonderful creatures is that they have evolved as part of Australia's environment. Their big feet and hopping action ensures that the fragile soil isn't broken down and eroded. The strongest are able to live through droughts and they can gain all the nutrients they need from the poor and scrubby vegetation. The balance between these animals and plants is a wonder of evolution.

So what did white settlers do with it when they first arrived? They shipped over sheep and cattle from Europe and there are now millions of them. Their hard hooves destroy the soil and to provide grass for them to eat, trees were felled, scrubs and bushes cleared and the Australian outback started to take on the completely unnatural look of a great prairie.

It has been a disaster. Australia is gradually turning into a desert but it is the kangaroos who are blamed for it. An animal that has lived in harmony with the land for millions of years is now called a pest and almost anyone can kill them.

The farmers claim they break down fences and destroy wheat crops. They drink water and eat grasses meant for cattle and sheep. But these excuses are manufactured. A six-year study at the University of New South Wales concludes: 'There was no evidence of a competitive effect of red kangaroos on sheep.' In other words, the presence of kangaroos does not cause sheep to grow or breed less well. And a four-year government study proved that 95 per cent of wheat crops are never visited by kangaroos. Furthermore, kangaroos are not even killed in areas where crops are grown but in the vast outback! But the killing goes on and it has now been turned into a money-making exercise.

Hunters go out at night in big four-wheel-drive trucks and sweep the countryside with powerful search lights. When one shines on a kangaroo, it will usually stop feeding, sit up on its haunches and stare at the light, completely blinded. The hunter then shoots it. He is supposed to shoot it through the head but frequently hits it in the throat, chest or body.

If the animal falls to the ground, the hunter drives over to it, cuts a gash in one of its back legs and then hangs it on a hook on the back of the truck. During all this, the kangaroo might still be conscious. Kangaroos that are only injured will limp off into the bush to die slowly.

If it's a female, the first thing the hunter does is to open the pouch and check to see if there's a joey inside. If it's a tiny joey he will stamp on it, club it or hit it against a rock – but not always to death. I have seen a joey stamped on but left writhing in the dirt as the hunter drove away.

Bigger joeys will be dragged out of the pouch and left to run off into the bush. Ones that are even older, the equivalent to teenagers, will have already run away in fear. All these young kangaroos die from cold and hunger or are killed and eaten by foxes and dingoes (a kind of wild dog). With no parent to protect them they are doomed.

At the end of the night there might be 30 or 40 kangaroos, dripping blood and hanging from the hooks on the hunter's truck. And he may well go out night after night, continuing the massacre for years on end.

The Australian Government says that the hunt is carefully supervised, but is this true? The shoot takes place at night, in very remote areas of a huge country and no official has the time or means to go out and check what's happening.

The animals are killed mostly for their skins, which are exported and used as leather to make clothing, trainers and other shoes. Most of it goes to Italy. Increasingly, the Australian Government is also trying to build an export trade in kangaroo meat.

Officially, nearly six million kangaroos could be shot in the year 2000. But this figure doesn't include the joeys who are also killed and so the real figure is several million higher. When you add on the millions more who are killed but aren't exported, as well as those killed by cars and lorries, the annual massacre of kangaroos is nearer to 12 million.

No one knows exactly how many kangaroos there are but when I did some media interviews in Australia, the meat-industry spokesmen said there were 30 million and a government department quoted 19 million. These are estimates of the species killed for meat. A further 17 species of kangaroo are endangered or vulnerable with very few remaining. When white settlers arrived in Australia, it is thought there were over 100 million kangaroos. Their numbers go up and down, depending on natural circumstances. If there hasn't been a big drought for several years, then there will be many more of them. When a drought happens, millions die. This is a natural process and ensures the fittest and healthiest – usually the biggest – survive to pass on their genes and build up the populations again.

The killers try to make the slaughter much more acceptable by calling it a 'cull' to control these numbers. The only way to cull animals that actually controls numbers is to destroy whole family groups. That isn't what the hunters do since they kill only the biggest. This allows the younger and smaller kangaroos, not necessarily the best animals, to mate and pass on what might be inferior genes. This is inevitably leading to serious problems for kangaroos, weakening their ability to survive and fight disease and threatening their existence.

Sealed fate

The massacre of seals off the coast of Canada is just as brutal as the killing of kangaroos. Again you hear the same old argument – that it is all the animals' fault.

In Canada's case, they claim that seals are destroying the few fish stocks that remain and are ruining the lives of fishermen. As you'll see in Chapter 9, these are the same fishermen who for years ignored all the advice they were given about overfishing and destroyed one of the biggest fishing industries in the world. Canadian fish stocks collapsed completely, throwing thousands of people out of work and causing huge environmental problems for other creatures who depend on fish. It was greed and ignorance that were responsible, not seals.

The truth is that there is money to be made out of seals but because the world is revolted by the slaughter, a reason has to be given for doing it.

The hunters' target is the harp and hooded seal pups which are born on the ice flows of Newfoundland off the north-eastern coast of Canada.

Seals are mammals and amazingly agile swimmers. Although they can dive as deep as 600 feet in search of food, and can stay under water for as long as 30 minutes, they always have to return to the surface to breathe. Throughout the winter, almost the entire surface of the sea is covered with ice and they have to make small holes in it to reach the air. Their sense of direction is so astute that they always return to the same tiny air hole without fail.

When they breed, they give birth to their pups on the ice floes (sheets of ice) and not in the water. This makes the young very vulnerable. The pups weigh about 9 kg at birth and are covered in a beautiful, creamy white fur – and it is this that the seal killers are after. These babies account for 80 per cent of their kill.

The little creatures are totally defenceless and have no

fear of the hunters. In any case, they are too young to escape to the water. They simply sit on the ice, looking with their huge brown eyes at these strange humans. The hunters are completely unmoved by this miracle of nature. Instead, they raise a long-handled pick and drive the spike into the baby's head. They may then hook the cub with a steel hook and drag it across the ice while it is still alive.

Observers have watched the slaughter and have seen baby seals clubbed to death in front of their mothers who have no way of protecting them. They have seen baby seals skinned alive and they have seen many seriously injured seals escape into the water where they will almost certainly die a slow and painful death.

A new trade has developed with the Far East to satisfy the demand for so-called 'medicines' to improve people's sex lives. Believe it or not, Canada sells seal penises. They are cut out, dried and eventually powdered and sold in preparations. There is a huge demand for them although there isn't a shred of scientific evidence to support the claim that they work, but that doesn't stop the barbaric trade from increasing every year.

Sometimes the flesh from the slaughtered seals is used to feed mink and foxes in Canadian fur farms, but more often they are left to rot on the ice.

Observers have seen the incredibly sad sight of mother seals carefully nosing, nudging and calling to the bloody, skinned corpses of their little ones, still able to identify them by their familiar odour.

All across the world, a brutal exploitation of wild animals takes place for profit. It is excused and supported by governments who often do so simply to win the votes of the killers. You may wonder how people can carry out such cruel acts. So do I, but I also find it disturbing that so many people are prepared to close their eyes, allowing the cruelty to happen and even pretending that it's necessary. All these barbaric assaults on animals would end tomorrow if we all opposed them and refused to buy the products of cruelty.

Hunting for profit is summed up by the words of one of the seal hunters, describing baby seals: 'They are dollar bills sitting out there on the ice waiting for me to collect them.' What to most people is a wonder of nature, a sight so beautiful and touching, is to him nothing more than another bottle of beer or a hamburger. I think that says it all.

Success Stories

- Viva! ran a very successful campaign to end the sale of kangaroo meat in Britain. They targeted supermarket chains and large catering companies one by one with days of action. Hundreds of local groups dressed as kangaroos and demonstrated outside the particular stores on the same days, gaining almost universal support from shoppers and creating lots of publicity for the poor kangaroos. All the supermarkets withdrew from the trade.
- Born Free launched the 'Elefriends' project to stop the mass destruction of elephants. It collected a massive 1.9 million-name 'Ivory Out' petition. In 1989 most of the world agreed to stop trading ivory and African and Asian elephants, and the sale of all elephant products was banned. Sadly, it's not a happy ending – yet. The ban has been partially lifted, so it is

legal to trade in ivory from some elephants.

- 'Elefriends' have stopped many animals being killed illegally by funding anti-poaching teams. They also move elephants from areas of conflict to safe havens within Kenya.

- An important conservation area for Asian elephants – the western forests of Thailand where national parks and sanctuaries cover 21,000 km² – is being protected by rangers. This project will help ensure this rare species (there are only 35,000–50,000 Asian elephants in the wild) has a secure future.

- The World Society for the Protection of Animals (WSPCA) have campaigned to reduce the number of bears being imprisoned for bile. The Chinese Government has agreed that no new cubs will be put into restrictive cages and that alternatives to bear bile will be researched (although alternatives already exist).

- The Whale and Dolphin Conservation Society (WDCS) persuaded Peru to stop hunting dolphins and porpoises, where as many as 20,000 were being killed each year.

- The Southern Ocean Whale Sanctuary (SOS), surrounding the Antarctic, was created in 1994 by the International Whaling Commission, following pressure from the WDCS, Greenpeace International and other groups. It protects three-quarters of the world's whales in their feeding grounds, including blue, fin, sei and humpback whales as well as the world's only large population of great whales that has not been seriously depleted by whaling – the Antarctic minkes. Other sanctuaries are being planned which would give the Antarctic whales full protection throughout their life.

- It is illegal to kill whales in this huge zone but one

country, Japan, defies the law. At the time of writing, a Greenpeace ship, the *Arctic Sunrise*, is off the coast of Antarctica to stop illegal whaling in this sanctuary. The brave crew are outwitting the Japanese killers from inflatable boats which zip back and forth between whaling ships, confounding the whaling crews and diverting them from their illegal hunt. Other tactics have included mounting a portable fire pump to the back of an inflatable and shooting a vertical spray of water eight metres into the air to block the vision of the harpooner to stop him from aiming at whales! Greenpeace have saved many whales with this type of awesome action.

Action for Animals

- Become an 'Elefriend'.
- Support the International Fund for Animal Welfare (IFAW)'s call for all ivory to be banned. Write to the Government's Minister for the Environment saying something like:

Your name
Your address

Minister for the Environment
Department of the Environment
Eland House
Bressenden Place
London SW1 5DV

Dear Minister for the Environment

I am against any lifting of the ban on ivory. During the 1980s, 700,000 elephants — half of Africa's elephants —

were slaughtered for ivory! This cannot be allowed to happen again. Any trade in ivory however 'limited' will lead to increased poaching. The UK government must take a leadership role in protecting this threatened species.

Yours sincerely
Your name

- Protest about the Canadian seal slaughter to:
  The High Commissioner
  The Canadian High Commission
  Grosvenor Square
  London W1X 0AB
- Put pressure on China to stop torturing bears and ask that the Government keeps its promise to not place cubs in restrictive cages and that alternatives to bear bile are used. Write to:
  The Ambassador of China
  Chinese Embassy
  49 Portland Place
  London W1N 3AH
- Join WSPA's 'Libearty' – a world campaign for bears – and give out leaflets, slap on stickers and plaster posters everywhere!
- Viva! needs your help to step up their successful campaign to stop kangaroos being massacred for meat and skin. Contact them *now* for sample letters, postcards, stickers and leaflets.
- Help keep the Southern Ocean Whale Sanctuary a haven for whales and stop the Japanese from hunting. Greenpeace International are calling on all governments of the world to contact Japan and demand an

end to the whaling. They need you to write to your MP (find out who she or he is by calling 020 7219 3000) with a letter like this:

Your name
Your address

Your MP's name (eg Mr P Nutt MP)
House of Commons
London SW1A 0AA

Dear MP's name (eg Mr Nutt)

I am writing to you about Japan's illegal whaling in the Southern Ocean Whale Sanctuary. Japan has resumed full-blown commercial whaling and is ignoring international law. I know that the British government has written to Japan asking for the whaling to stop but nothing has happened. Please urge the Prime Minister to do more to stop Japan whaling in the sanctuary.

Yours sincerely
Your name

Chapter 4

Behind Bars

Animals in Zoos and Circuses

It's one thing to feel strongly about animals – and many people say they do – but it's another thing to carry out your own research and then write, print and give out a leaflet around your school and town. But that's exactly what Ranie Richardson did. She goes to Botley CP School in Oxford, England. She was trying to get clear in her own mind whether zoos are a good or bad thing after visiting one and then reading arguments against captivity from Care for the Wild. Here's an extract from her leaflet:

'Zoos say that it is a good idea to keep animals because they breed endangered species and save them from extinction. Zoos say they are good for people's education and leisure, as they can study animals around the world. Many people like to see a real living animal at the zoo because you don't get to know the size and smell of it on TV. When animals' homes get destroyed and they don't have anywhere to live, zoos can provide a home. When animals' mums die, they can be fed and looked after in zoos.

'However, there are also strong arguments against this point of view. Many people have a good time in zoos but do the animals? Animals are cooped up in small cages and don't live their normal lifestyles. They are disturbed every minute of the day – people take photos and shout at them. Many animals such as tigers and polar bears go mental. They walk up and down their cages.

'After lots of research on the subject, I think that animals should be left in their natural environment.'

In those few words, Ranie has put her finger on most of the excuses used for keeping animals in zoos. If all these reasons were true there might – just might – be some excuse for having zoos. But the key purpose of zoos is to attract people in to look at the animals and make money from them.

To most zoos, their animals are commodities to be bought and sold. When they buy animals, they are often not too concerned about where they come from, their history or how much cruelty was involved.

Just think about this for a minute. We humans believe that freedom is probably the most important thing in the world. When someone does something really bad, what do we do to them? We take their freedom away by putting them in prison. We fight wars in the name of freedom and people are prepared to die for it. If freedom is so important to us, surely that should tell us that it is important to every creature – there's nothing different or special about us.

Instead, we cram little birds into cages, allow them no contact with their own kind, and make them sing for us. We hold farmed animals in dark and dingy hovels, and we take animals from the wild and put them in zoos. We then pretend they like it that way. They don't. Freedom is just as important to an animal as it is to us and in zoos and circuses they have no freedom and can lead only a shadow of their natural lives.

It's like claiming that prison is a magnificent way of protecting human beings. They can't be killed by traffic, they have central-heating, shelter and regular food. If they become ill there is always a doctor around. And they have no worries about survival. Oh yes? Do you want to try it for a few years?

The concept of zoos goes back to the nineteenth century when all kinds of animals were captured in the wild. No one cared about how they were caught, how many adults were killed to get a few babies, the misery of transporting them to a foreign climate halfway round the world and caging them up in tiny spaces so people could stare at them.

It was part of the culture of freak shows – letting people visit 'lunatic asylums' to laugh at the inmates and displaying two-headed babies or disfigured people such as the elephant man.

No one learns anything from a zoo other than what an animal looks like. But even that isn't accurate, because you will never see a cheetah dashing along at over 70 mph or a chimpanzee climbing high in a canopy of trees to gather fruit.

The record of zoos in running what they call 'captive breeding' programmes has been abysmal. This is where zoos try to breed endangered species with the aim of releasing them in the wild. Few zoos actually do it and those who do aren't very successful. A report by the World Society for the Protection of Animals and the Born Free Foundation revealed that by the mid-1990s, only two per cent of the world's 6000 threatened animal species were registered in zoo breeding programmes, and only 16 captive breeding programmes have ever successfully returned an endangered species to the wild. The main reason why animals are disappearing all over the world is because the places where they live are being destroyed. Even if zoos do become successful in breeding endangered animals, where are they going to release them?

So, if we want to save animals, supporting zoos is the wrong answer. The right way is to stop destroying the environment on which so many animals depend. The money spent on zoos should be poured into this.

However, the excuses used to defend zoos mean that millions of sad and dejected animals are kept in captivity. Across the world there are thousands of zoos – 300 in Britain alone, 1800 in the USA and when inspected many are found to be cruel and oppressive. It's usually the same list of abuses: enclosures too small; not enough access to water for those animals that depend upon it, such as crocodiles; and barren enclosures with no enrichment such as tree stumps for monkeys to climb.

On a recent visit to a Japanese zoo, big cats (such as lions) and bears were found chained in small metal cages; large primates (such as gorillas) were kept in tiny wire-mesh cages and other bears and a solitary African elephant were permanently tied near the zoo entrance so that visitors could have 'photo opportunities'.

One of the few enclosures that was anything like suitable contained macaque monkeys who seemed to be able to get on with their lives. Sadly, this wasn't the case – monkeys were regularly taken away and sent to laboratories for experiments to be carried out on them. The zoo owner insisted it was essential and would not hear that it was cruel and a betrayal of the animals in his care. It was also, of course, very profitable.

One of the clearest signs that something is wrong with a zoo animal is a condition called 'stereotypic behaviour'. This is when the animal repeats the same movement, such as pacing the same short path over and over again or weaving its head continually in a set pattern.

The words 'stereotypic behaviour' sound technical but what they actually mean is that the animal has had a complete mental breakdown. The conditions in which they live have driven them mad. Examples of this can be seen in zoos all over the world and a recent survey by the RSPCA confirmed this.

Here are just a few examples of what they found. In Belgium, a tiger continually paced its small enclosure and was extremely distressed by visitors standing in front of its cage. In Italy, monkeys were kept alone in tiny metal cages. In Portugal, gorillas and chimpanzees lived in small concrete pens with nothing to interest them. In Ireland, polar bears were kept in barren enclosures, going mad with boredom. In France, water deer were kept next to wolves, an animal that would kill and eat them in the wild. As a result, they were constantly terrified and used only a small amount of their enclosure.

All over Europe, similar instances of abuse were found, sometimes dozens of them in the same zoo. Zoos' owners know that it is rare species or babies that attracts visitors. But of course babies don't stay babies so continually have to be replaced. To make room, adult animals are dispensed with. The Captive Animals' Protection Society state that certain safari parks and zoos have admitted culling 'surplus' monkeys and supplying animals for vivisection. The Zoological Society of London, for example, has experimented on some unwanted animals, including marmoset monkeys and wallabies (Born Free Foundation, 'Zoo Fact Sheet 2'). Surplus ostriches and bison have been sold to farms to be reared for their meat.

Poor countries often have terrible zoos because they have no money to make life better for the animals, but rich countries can also treat their zoo animals terribly. The US, probably the world's wealthiest country, has some of the worst conditions for captive animals. Throughout the country, standards of care are extremely poor, even when those who run them have vast amounts of money.

Wild animals should not be in an unnatural environment where they are used to entertain bored people and make money for the company bosses. The fact that they are imprisoned in zoos is one of the reasons why 75 per cent of all the world's animals are in decline or facing extinction.

The story of an elephant called Pole Pole (pronounced Poly Poly, which means slowly) sums up the plight of some zoo animals. Pole Pole was born in Africa and for two years led a perfectly natural life, protected by her mother and her herd. One day in 1968, the poachers came and most of the herd were slaughtered, either for ivory or meat. Pole Pole was still very young, no more than a baby, and she was taken into captivity. She was given as a present to London Zoo by the Kenyan Government.

Before she left for England she was used in the film *An Elephant Called Slowly*, which was being made in Tsavo, one of Kenya's national parks – a huge natural area full of wild elephants and other animals. It also has an elephant sanctuary and it was here that Pole Pole was kept and she was adopted by an adult elephant called Eleanor.

Once the film was over, Pole Pole's happiness was brought to an end. She was torn away from her adoptive mother and transported to England where she spent years in a barren concrete enclosure, thousands of miles away from her friends and new mother and the heat and freedom of her natural home. Not surprisingly, she became disturbed and was called 'difficult and unpredictable'.

She started to take the misery out on other elephants – something unheard of in the wild – and bang her head against the wall of her enclosure. She injured herself and broke both her tusks. All these are signs of a very disturbed animal.

The biggest indication of mental breakdown was that she would rock constantly from side to side. As the few friends she had died or were moved to other zoos the situation became worse, and for the last years of her life she was completely alone. Eventually London Zoo tried to move her to Whipsnade Zoo and during the struggle she fell. She had lost the will to live and had to be put down. She was just 17 years old – still a teenager in elephant terms. (Elephants usually live to 60.) There are animals as unhappy and disturbed as Pole Pole all over the world.

When people talk about animals in captivity, they usually refer to food, water and housing and claim that if the animals have all these things they can't possibly want for anything else. They sometimes try to pretend that it is better for them than living in the wild.

The greatest animal watcher of all time was Charles Darwin, the man who worked out that humans were descended from animals. As well as being a vegetarian, he said that animals were capable of feeling the same range of emotions as us – fear, pain, anger but also love, affection, humour and jealousy. The one thing that is rarely taken into account in zoos is friendship and family ties. Animals are routinely torn away from these close bonds because it suits their 'owners'.

The ugliest show on earth

If zoos are bad, circuses are even worse. Circuses are held all over the world and many include animal acts. Magnificent bears are made to balance on seesaws, tigers and lions are forced to jump through hoops and elephants are made to sit up and beg. Is this the right way to treat magnificent wild animals?

From 1996 to 1998, the organisation Animal Defenders secretly went to work in circuses from Britain, France, Russia, Italy, Monte Carlo and Spain. You can be sure that their findings will be much the same all over the world – much worse in some cases.

During 7200 hours of observation, nearly 800 hours of video footage was recorded. The animals involved included tigers, lions, camels, elephants, horses, chimpanzees and llamas. Almost all circuses tour during the summer, often to other countries, and return to their permanent quarters in the winter. So there are two sets of problems – how the animals are kept when they are on the road and during the long winter months.

What the workers found was distressing. The film they made – *The Ugliest Show on Earth* (Animal Defenders, 1998) – was presented to an audience of journalists in London. There was a shocked silence as the packed cinema watched animals being locked up in tiny cages, and being beaten and abused.

When the circuses were on the road, the animals spent almost their entire lives in mobile cages called 'beast wagons'. The only exercise they were allowed occurred when they were moved from the wagons to perform in the circus ring. During the winter months they were mostly cooped up and often tethered in cramped, dingy dark quarters for months on end. Circus animals have only one purpose – to perform so that crowds will pay money to see them. Almost all their basic needs as intelligent animals are ignored.

The film showed that they suffer deprivation, stress and physical and verbal abuse. The abuse ranged from circus people trying to frighten them and making them cower to inflicting serious physical harm. One tigress was screamed at to such a violent degree that she urinated with fear. Other animals were whipped, punched, beaten with iron bars or broom handles, and had the bars of their cages banged.

One of the most well-known names in circus life in Britain is Chipperfield, and Mary Chipperfield is part of that family and was shown in the film. She and her husband both 'train' animals for circuses. The way Mary Chipperfield trained Trudy, a baby chimpanzee, brought tears to the eyes of almost everyone who witnessed it. This little animal would normally still have been clinging to its mother in a warm, loving family group, protected and looked after by the adult chimps. Chimps never beat their little ones.

Home for Trudy was a little, metal-barred dog kennel hardly any bigger than she was. Naturally, she hated going into it and when she refused she was beaten with a whip until she cried. Even that didn't stop this woman, who claimed she loved animals. She shouted at her and beat her some more saying she was glad she'd made her cry. The film showed the red wheals from the whip on Trudy's body.

The film also showed how Mary Chipperfield's husband, Roger Cawley, dealt with a sick elephant called Flora. She obviously found it difficult to keep going round the practice ring but she was whipped again and again to make her go faster. On another occasion, Cawley was shown beating Flora on the back, swinging a big metal bar with all his might and crashing it down on her. At the same time, another member of the Chipperfields, Charles, was beating her with a fibreglass rod.

As an indication of how much Roger Cawley loved animals, he had previously obtained monkeys from a safari park and sold them for vivisection (*Daily Mirror*, 28 January 1999).

Circuses are freak shows from another age and they should be treated like all freak shows – banned.

Dying to entertain you

Because dolphins are so intelligent and can be taught to perform tricks, they are a big attraction for the public. I'm going to talk about a type of big dolphin called killer whales (orcas) but much the same applies to all dolphins in captivity.

Orcas live in large family groups called 'pods', sometimes numbering more than 100. They stay together for life and have a very complicated way of communicating through sounds. While all orcas speak the same language, pods in different parts of the world have a different dialect – a bit like the difference between an American and English person. By analysing DNA from a tiny drop of blood or scrap of skin, it's possible to identify exactly which pod an orca came from.

Capturing orcas in the wild is a brutal and often deadly business with some being killed in the process. Try to imagine the incredible stress of being torn away from your family, forced into an alien environment and sometimes flown around the world in something you can't possibly understand. Once in captivity, these gentle creatures are a valuable commodity and are often sold from one marine park to another.

The first orcas were taken into captivity in 1961 and despite being such social animals, family ties and bonds are completely ignored. Orcas from different pods or even entirely different oceans are mixed together and the result is often severe stress. Calves are regularly separated from their mothers while they are still little more than babies and some orcas are even kept completely alone.

These are animals who can swim up to 100 miles in a single day, dive to 200 feet in search of fish and roam the ocean in complete freedom. In captivity, their world is usually a barren and sterile concrete pool where they live permanently eating nothing but dead fish.

Perhaps it's not surprising that animals that can live for 50 years or more in the wild rarely survive for longer than a few years in captivity. Of the 134 captured from the wild since 1961, 78 per cent are dead, most not reaching their sixth birthday. The death rate among new-born calves is also extremely high and of the 57 pregnancies that have happened in captivity, only 21 calves have survived. There are even examples of orcas trying to damage themselves. Smaller dolphins have actually killed themselves by continually swimming into the side of the pool, particularly after the death of a loved one.

The largest number of captive orcas are at Sea World in the USA – 20 out of a total of 50 in 2000. One of the inhabitants at Sea World is an orca called Corky. She was captured in 1969 from a pod off the coast of British Columbia and has been in captivity ever since. In April 2000, the *Sunday People* launched a campaign to free the orca. Whale and Dolphin Conservation Society campaigner Cathy Williamson said: 'We have tried to rescue Corky before but it has become much more urgent now. It's the 30th anniversary of her capture. The odds are heavily stacked against her surviving much longer. Keeping whales in captivity is very cruel. These animals are snatched from their families and the diversity of the ocean is replaced by a featureless tank. Unsurprisingly, many become depressed or develop chronic problems' (*Sunday People*, 2 April 2000).

An equally sad story involves Keiko, the star of the great film *Free Willy*. Everyone who saw that film went home with a feeling of satisfaction that this beautiful animal had been saved from the hands of brutal men who wanted to exploit him. Unfortunately the reality for Keiko was very different. Keiko was returned to the Mexico City amusement park that owned him and languished in a small tank seriously underweight and suffering from a contagious skin disorder (*Mail on Sunday*, 14 June 1998).

Success Stories

- Keiko, the orca star of *Free Willy* has at last been rescued. When the truth about the real 'Willy' was discovered, there was an international call for him to be released into the wild. Eventually Keiko was flown to the Oregon Coast Aquarium and then in 1998 to his native waters, where he now lives in a sea pen in the remote Westmann Islands in Iceland. Since then Keiko's keepers have continued to monitor his progress and hope to release him into the wild in mid-2000. The project is the first attempt to release a captive killer whale back into the wild. Keiko was about two years old when he was captured off Iceland in 1979; 21 years later he's going to be released to his natural home, back to the freedom of the sea and back to his family. It will be another major victory for animal rights groups and for humanity (see *Mail on Sunday*, 14 June 1998).

- About 120 out of 474 UK local authorites have banned circuses with animals from their land.

- Mary Chipperfield was convicted of 12 cruelty charges relating to Trudy in late 1997. Roger Cawley was 'convicted of whipping a sick elephant called Flora in order to "exercise" it' (*Daily Mail*, 6 February 1999). Although the court ruled that Trudy, the beaten and neglected chimpanzee, could be returned to the Chipperfields, 200,000 people wrote to the circus to prevent this from happening. Trudy is safe at a Dorset sanctuary, Monkey World.

- Born Free has rescued thousands of captive animals and has either given them homes in sanctuaries or has been able to rehabilitate them to return to where they belong – in the wild. For example, in 2000 they helped close Noah's Ark Zoo, Italy, where animals lived in barren cages in a terrible state (*Wildlife Times*, Spring 2000). Homes were found for hundreds of reptiles and several ponies and donkeys and many animals were given veterinary treatment. Born Free also find homes for bears and tigers who are thin and going insane in their sterile environments.

- Corky has survived longer than any other orca in captivity. The Free Corky Project is calling for her return to the ocean while she still has the chance to live a natural life. The project's mascot is Corky's Great Freedom Banner, created by thousands of children around the globe. It is now the longest banner in existence, stretching over two and a half kilometres and made up of 14,000 individually painted or sewn patches. It represents the call of thousands of people around the world for Corky to be set free. The banner is still growing as the Whale and Dolphin Conservation Society's freedom campaign continues.

Action for Animals

- Don't go to circuses with animals, zoos, safari parks, aquaria or dolphinaria. Enjoy yourself at a non-animal circus instead. Urge your friends to do the same.
- Educate a school! If you know of a school that takes children to zoos or circuses, ask to see the head teacher or get a group such as Animal Defenders or Born Free to contact them.
- If you do visit a zoo go as an investigator. Contact Born Free for a checklist of what to look out for and a questionnaire to complete; also take lots of photos or video footage and send all your evidence to them.
- Find out if your local council has banned animals in

circuses from their land. If not write to them and to the letters page of your local paper.
- Send for the Animal Defenders Circus Action Pack with leaflets, petitions and video, *Circus Madness*.
- Urge your MP to ban animals from circuses. Here's a sample letter:

Your name
Your address

Your MP's name (eg Mr Richard Head MP)
House of Commons
London SW1A 0AA

Dear MP's name (eg Mr Head)

Using animals for 'entertainment' in circuses is cruel and unjustifiable. For example, elephants in the wild travel 20 miles a day, living in family groups. In the circus they spend 60 per cent of their time chained by a leg, barely able to move and are very lonely. Lions and tigers are imprisoned 90 per cent of the time in small cages on the backs of lorries called beastwagons. Bears are shut away for a similar amount of time. These animals are trained using sticks, metal-tipped poles and whips and are often beaten.

Tradition can't justify such misery – nothing can. Please help end it and support a ban on animals in circuses.

Yours sincerely
Your name

- If an animal circus comes to town politely ask shops displaying posters to remove them and explain why. Distribute leaflets from Animal Defenders, Animal Aid and Born Free. Write to your newspaper and ask people not to go.
- If you know of animals in poor condition at a zoo contact Born Free or the Captive Animals' Protection Society.
- Cry Freedom! Get arty and add your work to the Great Freedom Banner to end the imprisonment of Corky and all orcas. Contact the Whale and Dolphin Conservation Society (WDCS) for info.
- Write to or email Sea World to ask that Corky be set free and reunited with her long-lost family. A sample letter could go:

Your name
Your address

Sea World Head Office
email: shamu@seaworld.org
Director of Zoological Operations
Sea World Inc.
7007 Sea World Drive
Orlando, FL 32821 807
USA

Dear Director

I'm shocked to discover that Sea World own 40 per cent of the world's captive orcas. These mighty animals are not suited to confinement – as the catalogue of failed pregnancies, illnesses and early deaths have shown. Instead of freedom to travel 160 km a day, or to dive to 60 m deep in the ocean, Sea World keeps these complex and highly intelligent mammals in small, bare concrete tanks.

Orcas are intensely social animals, yet in captivity family ties are broken and calves usually separated from their mothers. In the wild, a calf remains with its mother for life.

Sea World has still not released Corky. Surely after 30 years, Corky deserves a chance of freedom? A plan to release Corky has been proposed to Sea World by Dr Paul Spong, a well-known and respected researcher who studies orcas in the wild and who knows Corky's family group (who she can be reunited with). The plan has the support of many conservation groups, including the Whale and Dolphin Conservation Society. Please ensure Sea World adopts this plan and frees Corky soon.

I look forward to hearing from you shortly.

Yours sincerely
Your name

- Adopt a whale or dolphin with the WDCS. You'll receive a certificate, photo, sticker and newsletter – and know you are helping rescue captive animals and making the oceans a safer place for all wild creatures.

'As we've reached the new millennium, when we are overwhelmed with choice of entertainment, we must ask ourselves what possible pleasure can be found in watching animals degraded into performing tricks completely unnatural to them. I am horrified at the suffering of circus animals. It is inexcusable this oudated "freak show" should continue.'
Pam St Clement, *EastEnders*

'What right do we have to put these precious creatures through unbearable, unspeakable torment all for profit and self-gain? This is barbarism and deception at its highest form. The public should know the truth about circuses.'
Kim Basinger, actress

'The animal circus is a relic of a bygone era and has no place as a form of modern entertainment.'
Sir Elton John, singer/songwriter

Chapter 5
Blinded by Science
Experiments on Animals

Lisa Porter, 14, of Birmingham, wasn't convinced that medical experiments on animals were necessary. After a visit to her school by a speaker who was totally in support of animal testing, Lisa decided to do some digging around.

'The guy who came to our school to talk about animal experiments was one of those people who you trust straight away. He seemed completely honest and open, the kind of man who wouldn't lie. I realised he believed everything he said to us and as a result he had the class eating out of his hand, if you know what I mean. He certainly had me convinced. It was when he showed the video that I started to have doubts.

'I'd seen a few leaflets and posters around the place and on animal-rights stalls in the high street so I knew that some pretty horrible things are done to animals. But of course, they might well be necessary – I just didn't know. What I did know was that it wasn't all sweetness and light. But the video we were shown was like a holiday camp for happy critters. All it showed was some blood being taken with a syringe, rats and mice in glass tanks and lots of people saying how important it was to test medicines on animals.

'The presenter on the video was cool – pretty, young and very friendly. She smiled all the time and had a gorgeous beagle dog with her, who licked her and wagged its tail every time she spoke to it. It was all too good to be true.

'That weekend, I went to one of the stalls in town and asked the people who ran it about animal experiments. They gave me loads of leaflets and let me borrow a short video. It had been filmed inside one of the biggest animal experiment labs in the UK. It was made secretly by a man who had worked there.

'Even in the first few seconds I began to feel a sense of horror. The video began with dogs – these were beagles as well – in their cages. They were tiny cages, metal bars all round and there was absolutely nothing inside – no toys, no bedding, nothing but barren steel. The poor things looked terrible. You could tell by the way they were slumped, their eyes sad and drooping, that they were very unhappy.

'What happened next was terrible. You see a man's hand open the cage door and the beagle inside suddenly looks absolutely petrified. It cowers in the back of the cage, getting as far away from the man as it can, and lifts its paw as if to say: "Please don't do this to me." The look on its face is one of complete horror.

'The man reaches inside, grabs it by the scruff of its neck and drags it out of the cage, swearing at it. He swings it up onto a table and tries to find a vein to take a blood sample. The beagle doesn't keep still and so he shakes it viciously making it yelp and cry. He keeps trying to take a blood sample, jabbing at the dog's leg time after time, making it cry out with every stab of the needle. He still can't find the blood and shakes the dog again viciously and then punches it in the face with his fist more than once. Another man can be seen watching and all he does is laugh. It made me feel sick in my stomach. And all this just for a blood sample!'

Your mum's life, your little sister's life or the life of a rat or a dog – that's the choice you're given whenever people talk about 'vivisection' (experiments on living animals). Put like that, what else can you do but agree with it?

But that's not the choice at all. In fact, it's nothing more than emotional blackmail. There is a very strong argument that testing on animals isn't necessary and isn't even good science. As we'll see later, it has delayed cures for serious illnesses and is actually responsible for killing people. But still the torture and slaughter of animals goes on, affecting three million in Britain every year. They seem to care so little about animals that another six million are killed every year just because they're 'surplus to requirements'. Around the world over 100 million animals die every year.

It isn't just the pain of being experimented on – their whole lives are sad and miserable. No matter how often we're told that laboratory animals are well protected and are looked after in a kind way, every time someone gets inside a laboratory with a secret camera they film sickening scenes which should shame us all.

The usual claim is that all laboratory animals are protected by laws. That's very misleading. There are very few laws to protect them and most are there to protect the 'vivisectors' (those who carry out the experiments) so they can't be charged with cruelty to animals.

In a laboratory you can do just about anything you want to an animal, no matter how painful or cruel. You can:

- Infect an animal with lethal viruses and watch it die without providing any relief, no matter how long it takes.
- Cut animals open or cut off their limbs just to see how their bodies work.
- Damage their brains with severe blows to the head, starve them, lock them in solitary confinement until they go mad – just so long as you claim you are carrying out 'psychology tests'.
- Hold them against red hot metal plates or pour boiling water over them – so long as you say it's for 'burns research'.
- Forcibly pour poisons, burning chemicals and corrosive fluids down their throats – so long as you call it 'product testing'.
- Gas them, burn them or fire bullets through them and call it 'warfare research'.

Why is so much suffering allowed? The usual answers are: it's necessary to make sure the food we eat and the products we use are safe; and we will die from horrible illnesses unless animals are used for medical research.

Next time you go into a supermarket, look along the shelves where the polishes and cleaners are kept. Probably every one of those products has been tested on animals – not just one or two animals but hundreds of them. Weed-killers, paint ingredients, washing powders, food additives – the list is almost endless.

It's called 'toxicity testing' but what it really means is poisoning. The products are force fed to animals, sprayed onto them or injected into them, and then the testers watch and wait, for weeks or even months. The animals will almost certainly suffer great pain but they will receive no painkillers or anaesthetics. Eventually, many of them will die. Those who don't die will either be killed or put back into the cages for use in other experiments.

One of the cruellest tests is called the Draize test and it is mostly rabbits who are used. Their heads are held in stocks so they can't move and chemicals are dripped into their eyes. Some of these chemicals will burn or irritate the eye and cause painful inflammation but the rabbits can do nothing about it. Why rabbits? Not because they are the animals most like humans but simply because they have big eyes and few tears to wash the chemicals away.

Medical experiments can be equally as painful. Most are carried out without anaesthetics and even when anaesthetics are used, there is no guarantee that painkillers will be given when the animals come round. Can you believe that to give anaesthetics to animals you don't need to be a trained anaesthetist? And you don't have to be a vet or even a surgeon to perform something as complicated as brain surgery on a monkey.

Another claim that vivisectors often make is that only mice and rats are used – as if they don't feel pain. But it's not true. Just about every animal you can think of is used in experiments – cats, ferrets, gerbils, hamsters, pigs, sheep, horses, birds, dogs – the list goes on and on. Why do you think it's usually beagle dogs that are used? Because they are friendly, gentle and kind and don't fight back! What a way to repay them.

The one animal that vivisectors never want to talk about is the monkey, our distant relative. A few are bred here but most are imported from abroad and some are caught in the wild. Monkeys live in close family groups. They feed together, play together and sleep together, and grooming each other is an important part of their day. Imagine the utter fear and confusion when these wonderfully intelligent creatures are caught in nets, torn away from their family group and forced into tiny cages. Many will die before they even reach a laboratory, often from suffocation or thirst. When they do arrive at their final destination – the laboratory where they will be experimented on and killed – they are usually kept in barren and sterile cages, terrified and alone.

Of mice, not men, women or children...

The excuse for using animals in medical experiments is that it's the only way of finding new drugs. This is simply not true. Animals are used because they have always been used, because they are plentiful and because it's quicker and easier than other methods. However, animals are unlike us in so many ways that the results are often useless. For example:

- If you give morphine to humans, they go to sleep. It does the opposite to cats.
- Aspirin cures our headaches and other pains but it damages the unborn babies of mice and rats.
- The contraceptive pill can sometimes cause blood to thicken and clot in women. It makes a dog's blood thinner.

There are lots more examples like this and even the diseases animals get are not the same as those experienced by humans.

Heart disease in people is mostly caused by eating animal products – meat, fat, butter and other dairy products. These cause the blood vessels to clog up. No matter how much of this stuff you feed to a dog, it doesn't block its arteries and yet they still use dogs for research into heart disease. Rats and mice get cancer but not the same types of cancer as humans yet still they're used for cancer research.

To 'solve' this problem vivisectors try to create the diseases artificially. For heart disease, they cut dogs open and tighten wires around the blood vessels leading to their hearts. For cancer, they inject cancer cells directly into the animals, sometime into their eyes or brains. Having given them a disease that they would never naturally have, vivisectors then attempt to find a cure.

It probably doesn't come as a great surprise to discover that drugs obtained from animal experiments often go wrong when they're taken by people. Drugs that have been developed to cure one disease have often caused a totally different one, and no one had any idea this would happen despite poisoning thousands of animals to prove that the drug was safe.

Thrown off the scent

Medical knowledge has grown over the years but most of the important discoveries have nothing to do with torturing animals. In fact animal experiments have often thrown us off the track and actually prevented us from finding out what causes some diseases.

- For years we were told that smoking doesn't cause cancer because it didn't cause it in dogs when they were forced to inhale cigarette smoke for months on end.

- One of the most deadly substances to humans is asbestos, once used in lots of houses for insulation. Just inhaling a tiny amount can eventually lead to cancer. But it doesn't have the same effect on animals, so our knowledge was delayed and people were placed at risk for years longer than they need have been.
- Alcohol is a poison and can cause serious damage to the liver but again knowledge was delayed because in experiments alcohol didn't have the same effect on animals.

So why do they do it? Why are animals the innocent tools of so many medical experiments?

Curiosity killed the cat

There are many reasons. The starting point was France in the nineteenth century. 'Learned men' would cut up fully conscious living dogs and cats – no anaesthetic, no pain relief – in front of an audience curious to see how their bodies worked. The cruelty is almost unimaginable but that started a trend. Of course other people, who also wanted to show themselves as being just as educated and knowledgeable, did similar experiments. And so vivisection was born.

Textbooks were written based on animal experiments and it became an automatic part of students' training. Before long, scientists who wanted to improve their careers would carry out experiments and publish the results. That became the accepted way of doing things, the only acceptable way to improve your career – and it still is. In medical colleges and universities, all the lecturers were taught to do animal experiments and so they teach their students exactly the same methods.

Gradually, a huge industry was formed: the researchers themselves, their assistants, people in charge of the animals. Animal breeding companies started up and with them came the manufacturers of cages, transport boxes, holding devices and all the scalpels and instruments that were necessary. Feed manufacturers were needed, vets and animal transporters, until we reach the present where a vast industry employing thousands, possibly millions, of people exists. Animal experiments are how these people make their living and their profits. Killing animals works extremely well for them.

Drug culture

Probably the greatest power of all is in the hands of drugs manufacturers (not illegal drugs but the kind your doctor prescribes) – the pharmaceutical companies. They are some of the biggest companies in the world and make huge profits. Each year, between them, they pocket $161 thousand million, most of it from selling drugs obtained from animal experiments. Why on earth would they want to change anything?

They keep on pouring out more and more drugs, most of them no different to the drugs that already exist. When one company launches a new drug, all the other drug companies watch and wait to see how successful it is. If it looks like it will make big bucks for its owner, all the other companies start working on their own version so they can cash in on the bonanza. There are copyright laws which stop them directly copying the original drug so they have to make their own version which is almost the same but with minor variations. One of the first things they do is to begin experimenting on animals. These drugs are known as 'me too' drugs because most of the companies when they see a new pill shout 'me too, me too!'

It has nothing to do with making people well but everything to do with making profits. It is estimated that 70 per cent of all the animals killed in medical experiments are killed for 'me too' drugs – for greed.

The independent medical organisation called the World Health Organisation, made up of doctors from all over the world, reckon that virtually all the known diseases and illnesses could be treated with just 200 different drugs. But still the pharmaceutical companies keep turning out new ones.

In all there are about 18,000 pills and potions and as many as 4000 animals have been used for every one. It's estimated that 250 million animals have been killed in the last 50 years in this industry.

So many animals are used because companies want to protect themselves. If someone who takes one of their pills becomes ill because of it and takes the company to court, the first thing the manufacturers say is: 'We carried out all the necessary safety tests and they showed the pill was safe to take.' The courts usually accept that as a proper defence and so the companies keep on using animals.

Despite this, not only do prescription drugs make some people very ill, they can kill them. Drugs prescribed by doctors are the fourth biggest cause of death in Europe and America. It comes after heart disease, cancer and road deaths. So much for safety! So much for animal experiments!

The usual cry from vivisectors is 'TINA' – There Is No Alternative. This is the same excuse that was used to justify slavery, child labour, oppression of women, whaling, otter hunting and dozens of other cruel practices. In fact there are plenty of alternatives to animal experiments including tests on human cells (we're made up of millions of them), computer simulations, studies on dead people (who gave their consent) and, most important of all, studies of living people.

Cleanliness is close to healthiness

One hundred years ago and more, poverty, poor housing, dirty drinking water, bad working conditions, filth and squalor ensured that many people died from infectious diseases. Changing those conditions meant that people were much healthier and lived longer. This did far more to save people from the ten most infectious diseases than all the drugs and vaccines put together.

When vivisectors claim that their vaccines wiped out killer diseases, they always forget to tell you that almost all these diseases had almost disappeared before the vaccines were developed. The success wasn't due to animal experiments but through studying real people to find out what caused the diseases.

Only by studying people did we learn that smoking causes cancer. Only by studying people did we learn that fatty animal foods cause heart disease.

Despite years of animal experiments, death rates from cancer and heart disease have hardly altered. In fact they're increasing and are still the two biggest killers in the Western world. This is crazy when they can mostly be prevented by healthy living. But of all the money spent on health – billions and billions – almost nothing is spent on prevention. Of course, no one makes huge profits from giving advice but they can make a fortune if they find a drug that works. While people are waiting for that to happen, they go on dying unnecessarily.

The argument against animal experiments isn't just about it not being good science. Many people believe it is wrong for moral reasons. If you've ever had anything to do with animals, you'll know that their lives are every bit as important to them as our lives are to us. They don't want to be terrified, locked up, tortured and killed any more than we do. The terrible thing is that they have no idea what's being done to them and why.

How can it be justified? If it's because we're stronger than them, that's just bullying. If it's because they are supposed to be less intelligent than us, then why don't we experiment on babies, people who are brain damaged or who have severe learning difficulties? The logic would be the same.

Vivisection is not just a choice between animals and people, it's a choice between humane research and that which is cruel and ineffective. One thing is certain, the day will come when we look back on this mass torture of innocent creatures and we will be just as shocked as we are when we think about the millions of people who were forcibly taken from their countries and sold into slavery. It has to end and you can help that come about.

Respect, not dissect

Some schools still practise dissection – the cutting up of dead animals, or parts of them. In the UK sheep eyes and lungs, cow hearts, chicken feet, whole rats and insects are sometimes used. In the US, add chipmunks, cats, frogs and foetal pigs to the list. The argument given by some teachers is that dissection enhances 'scientific thinking' and makes it easier to investigate the internal structure of animals. However, many teachers now believe that dissection distracts students because they often find it disgusting. It also encourages students to think of animals as disposable objects, instead of instilling a respect for life.

In the UK, you don't have to take part in dissection. Teachers aren't allowed to make you or mark you down for refusing. (Of course some may not tell you this!) There are lots of alternatives available, ranging from detailed models and computer simulations to films of animals in their natural habitat.

Success Stories

- The British Union for the Abolition of Vivisection (BUAV) and other groups have lobbied hard to end the testing of cosmetics in the UK. They persuaded more than 80 per cent of the public that these tests are indefensible and thousands of letters were sent to politicians. Letter writing can work! In 1997 the government announced a ban and about 3000 animals have been saved each year.
- The BUAV had a fantastic UK victory in 1999. After campaigning for years to stop the notorious LD50 test –

which involves force-feeding drugs, pesticides, household products and so on to animals to find the dose at which half of them are poisoned to death – it was banned for toxicity testing. Although non-toxicity tests remain, more than half the experiments have ended.

- Animal Aid have saved thousands of animals by issuing a Humane Research Donor Card in 1991. By carrying the card you show your willingness to allow your tissue to be used for medical research, instead of live animals. The Dr Hadwen Trust is helping fund the first centralised Human Tissue Bank to store and distribute human tissues to scientists throughout Britain. This will also save tens of thousands of animals and, through more accurate research, people too!

- The Dr Hadwen Trust and the Humane Research Trust have funded many successes in non-animal research. For example, computer modelling experts at Glasgow University have improved treatments for cancer of the nervous system in children and cancer of the immune system. Usually cancer therapies were tested on mice by implanting tumours but the humane approach has rendered the animal tests obsolete.

- Hillgrove Farm, which bred cats for vivisection, was closed down by determined campaigners. They turned up week after week to protest outside the Oxfordshire unit and after two years succeeded in ending the cruelty. Safe homes were found for the 800 cats.

- In March 2000, the UK's largest primate importation and quarantine centre for laboratory monkeys, Shamrock (GB) Ltd, was forced to close following a 15 month campaign by local protest group, Save the

Shamrock Monkeys. The farm could hold up to 300 macaque monkeys at any one time in tiny cages, before being sold on to labs throughout Europe. During the farm's 46 years of trading, hundreds of thousands of monkeys had been sold for experiments, after they had been transported from countries such as the Philippines and Mauritius.

- Students all over the UK have had a wonderful victory! They have worked with organisations such as Animal Aid to stop dissection being required by any examination board. Individual teachers may still ask you to dissect but you can resist! Here's an example of what to do. Cate Rapley of Stoke on Trent was asked to dissect a rat when she was 15. She says:

'Rats were placed out on wooden boards and we were told to lie them flat on their backs and hammer pins through their paws.

'I refused to take part but my friend, Kathryn, felt pressurised. When she cut the rat open she found that she was pregnant. We were very upset and so was the rest of the class. It brought home how dissection tries to make you dismissive of animal life. But animals do matter and we decided to make a stand.

'I wrote to Animal Aid for information, leaflets and petitions and gave them out. My class collected signatures from about half the school. We asked to see the head teacher and took along the petitions and a book of alternatives to dissection. She listened carefully and asked lots of questions and thankfully we were prepared! Soon afterwards, the life science teacher said that anyone who didn't want to dissect could choose alternatives – that was the end of cutting up innocent animals in my class!'

Action for Animals

- Refuse to dissect. Contact Animal Aid for a free pack with leaflets, petitions and information on alternatives.
- Boycott companies who test on animals. Although cosmetics tests are banned in the UK, companies still test in other countries and then import those products into Britain. Contact the BUAV for their free *Little Book of Cruelty-Free* which lists about 50 companies who don't test cosmetics, toiletries or household products in any country.
- Look out for the BUAV 'leaping rabbit' symbol on products throughout Europe – this means that they are not tested on animals.
- Return products that have been tested and ask for a refund – this certainly gets the message across! (If you're not sure if a product is tested, write to the company and ask.)
- Encourage your local chemists and hairdressers to sell cruelty-free products.
- Take responsibilty for your health so you're less likely to become ill! Go vegetarian – it reduces your chances of getting heart disease, cancer and about 60 other diseases! Contact Viva! for a free *Go Veggie with Viva!* pack.
- Don't support charities which fund animal research. Contact PETA for their booklet *Health Charities: Helping or Hurting* which lists medical charities which test on animals – and those who don't. How about a letter along the lines of:

Your name
Your address

Director General
Charity's name and address

Dear Director General

I'm shocked that your charity funds painful experiments on animals and urge you to stop. As animals' bodies are so different to humans', your aim would be best achieved by funding educational campaigns and non-animal research – some of which you already support.

Please follow the lead of other charities by focusing your research solely on non-animal methods. I will not donate to your charity while you continue to vivisect. I look forward to your reply.

Yours sincerely
Your name

'As one who did not dissect in school and who is now a vet and trains doctors-to-be, I can state that dissection is totally unnecessary for the biologically minded pre-college student.'
Professor Nedim Buyukmihci, University of California, School of Veterinary Medicine

'The mode of action of drugs is very complicated, so it is regrettable that most of the extensive literature on animal experimental work is irrelevant to curing humans since many species respond in a very different manner from humans.'
JS Beck and MCK Browning, University of Dundee, Department of Pathology and Biochemical Medicine

'...conflicting animal tests have often delayed or hampered advances in the war against cancer and have never produced a single substantial advance either in the prevention or treatment of cancer.'
Dr Irwin Bross, Rosewell Park Memorial Institute for Cancer Research

'Animal-based research is not only cruel, it represents one of the biggest and most grotesque blunders in medical history.'
Dr Andre Menache, President, Doctors and Lawyers for Responsible Medicine

Chapter 6

Creature Comforts

Companion Animals at Home

There's hardly a person in the world who hasn't had something to do with an animal at some time in their life. Cats, dogs, rabbits, gerbils – there are dozens of different kinds that people love to have as friends. Wendy John, 16, met a particularly handsome animal when she was on holiday.

'Our whole family went to Turkey on holiday and had a great time. There were all the usual things I like to do – lovely golden beaches, boats to sail in, huge mountains and lots of sunshine.

'We stayed in a village called Hisaronu and our hotel wasn't anything like the ones you see in holiday brochures – big skyscraper blocks with a concrete swimming pool. Ours was only two floors high and right on the edge of the village. Outside my room, a dog was tied to a tree on a long chain.

'He was there for the first four days and then I realised he was probably going to be there for the whole holiday. Men came out of the kitchens and gave him piles of meat and bones but he was never let off the chain. They told me he was a watchdog who would bark if a thief came prowling around at night. It didn't do much good because

101

people were always coming back late from the disco and no one took any notice of his barking.

'He was probably the most beautiful dog I've ever seen. He had a big broad face, amber coloured eyes and reminded me of a wolf. I decided to call him Barney. One day I asked if I could take him for a walk. The chain was untied, I took hold of it and off we went at about 100 miles an hour – Barney running and me being dragged behind. I couldn't stop even if I'd wanted to.

'It became a regular thing and I took him every day, usually to the pine woods where there were no other people. He loved it. But one day, as we got back to the hotel, he got off his chain and ran off into the village. I followed behind, panicking like crazy but all he did was go round all the streets looking for other dogs. When he found them he barked and growled and they all backed down. He really was top dog.

'Just before the end of the holiday someone told me that in the winter, the hotel owners usually shot their guard dogs so they didn't have to feed them. In the spring they picked up a new one – a stray. The man at our hotel said he had no intention of shooting Barney, but I don't know if I believed him.

'Anyway, when I got home I so missed Barney that I persuaded my folks to let me have a dog. I went to a rescue place and got a wonderful big black dog called Charlie. So some good came out of it.'

Almost as long as humans have lived together in groups, it seems they have made companions out of animals ('companion' is a better word than 'pet' which makes animals sound like toys). In this chapter, I'm not going to provide you with an instruction manual of how to look after different animal friends, there are already hundreds of books which do that. Instead, I want to open your mind to the needs of animals. Unless we are able to look at an animal's needs and desires with understanding, it will always be a lopsided arrangement and the result will often be a distressed, unhappy and frustrated animal. The pointers I give here with a few of the most popular animals apply in different ways to all animals.

The two most common animal companions all over the world are dogs and cats. No one knows exactly how this relationship began but historians have tried to turn it into a practical arrangement with no emotion. They say the reason probably stems from when humans first became farmers and stored grain for the winter. Rats and mice came along to help themselves and this attracted wild cats which could feed on the rodents. This suited humans and cats so they stayed.

The reason why humans chose dogs to be companion animals is less clear but one explanation is that wolves began to scavenge around human settlements and were eventually adopted. The dogs that you and I know are all descended from wolves. Whatever the practicalities, I suspect the reason people lived with animals centuries ago was the same as they do now – they liked them!

What is extraordinary is why people changed these beautiful animals into such different-looking creatures. Imagining that a tiny Yorkshire terrier or a huge St Bernard or Great Dane was once a wolf is very hard.

Over the centuries, dogs were bred selectively to produce a particular size for a particular purpose, or to strengthen certain characteristics. The Irish wolfhound was bred to be big and strong and fast so that it could kill wolves – something, of course, that would never have happened without human interference.

Fox terriers were bred very small so they could get down a fox earth and attack the fox in its home – another 'wonderful' invention of humans. Spaniels have been developed to sniff out animals and birds hiding in bushes and clumps of grass so that they can be shot at. Pointers will stop and point their noses at a hidden animal, their tail going back stiff and in a straight line. By looking at the direction in which the dog is pointing, the hunter knows where to aim his gun.

So much of dog breeding was to do with killing other animals. Bull terriers were used for bull and bear baiting, where these huge creatures were tied up and the dogs set on them – for fun!

Much of this selective breeding has been a disaster for dogs. Most pedigrees (a specific breed such as a full Labrador) have inherited weaknesses. It might be a weak back or the fact that they die young. Some, like Pekinese or bulldogs, have been bred to have short stubby noses and deep chests. The result is that they suffer from asthma. Some are hairless or so tiny that they are not much bigger than a rat. With rabbits, some have been bred with ears so long that they can't walk without standing on them.

Similar breeding patterns have been imposed on cats but compared to dogs, they seem to have retained more of their natural looks and behaviour. If you look closely at a tabby cat, she or he looks similar to a wild cat, the caffre cat of Egypt, that some experts believe is the ancestor of all domestic cats.

Most companion animals are loved, respected and are

a part of the family. They can include any manner of creature – from rabbits to rats, hamsters to horses. Some, sadly, are appallingly treated by individuals and this is a complete betrayal of the bond which exists between people and animals.

Animals will give love unconditionally. They don't care what you look like, what colour you are, whether you're clever or stupid, fat or thin, smelly or fragrant. They will give you everything they have and ask for very little in return. Of course that makes them easy to abuse by the few people in this world who mistake cruelty for strength. To subject any creature to abuse – whether human or another animal – because it is not as strong as you is not a sign of strength but one of enormous weakness.

The result of this is some pretty horrific statistics. In the US 13 million abused, stray or unwanted cats and dogs are put to death each year. In Britain, it's estimated that every year, new homes are found for about 150,000 animals who have been abandoned, abused or neglected by their owners. This doesn't include the 500,000 strays who are roaming the streets at any one time. When you add to the total about 365,000 perfectly healthy dogs that are destroyed by vets, some so-called animal shelters and local councils – 1000 every day of the week – it's a very disturbing picture.

You can almost guarantee that there are similar statistics in every country, the number of animals increasing or decreasing according to the human population.

Pet shop toys

Many so-called pets are bought on a whim, with probably less thought given to the purchase than to a new pair of trainers. When people start to find out the cost of feeding an animal, paying for someone to look after it if they go away, or vet's bills, they simply dump it.

What seems almost incredible is that, despite the vast number of abandoned animals, so many people still insist on buying particular breeds, just as though they were fashion accessories or toys, from breeders or pet shops.

Whenever pet shops are inspected, many problems are found. A survey discovered that animals are often treated just as though they have no feelings: their cages are too small; the conditions dirty and unhygienic; babies are taken away from their mothers too soon; too many animals are crammed together; and staff often don't know how to look after them! Pet shops also encourage impulse buys from owners who are irresponsible or incapable of giving an animal proper care. If the animals weren't displayed, often huddled pathetically in the shop window, not so many would be bought and not so many would be bred.

Give shops that sell animals the elbow and buy all your companion's needs from one which doesn't sell living creatures. If you decide to get a companion, there are thousands in rescue centres and sanctuaries who will make beautiful and wonderful friends. You will also be providing space so that another abused, neglected or lost creature can be given a home.

Friend or gaoler?

There are big questions hanging over how you should keep your companion animal. I believe that at the heart of our attitude towards them must be respect for their needs. They have evolved over millions of years and have instincts and abilities which need to be exercised and used.

Puppy love

Dogs have a sense of smell that is quite amazing. Their world is largely composed of smells as this is their most finely tuned sense. I have watched my own dogs padding down a lane quite happily, sniffing the air and happy to be alive. Ahead of them a rabbit has crossed the path in a sudden burst of speed, its tail bobbing away. Neither has seen it but when they've reached the spot where the rabbit crossed, both have picked up the scent immediately and followed it. This happens all the time.

One of my dogs, Lulu, has a lot of spaniel in her and her habits are typical of this breed. Some walks such as neatly clipped parks and city streets bore her while others excite her enormously. Her favourite walk is in open countryside such as the English South Downs where there are few people but lots of hawthorn bushes, bramble patches and clumps of docks, nettles and thistles. Off she goes, sniff, sniff, sniffing from bush to bush and her tail never stops wagging. When she picks up the scent of a wild animal, it lashes her into a frenzy of pleasure.

She hardly even notices the animals she's smelling and never chases them. Her joy is simply that of sniffing them.

My other dog Charlie is big and black with lots of Labrador in him. He has little interest in Lulu's pastimes. His greatest delight is to run with horses. He is always the leader, constantly looking back to check the distance between them, always able to produce an additional burst of speed in order to stay ahead. A horse in full gallop with

Charlie in the lead, urging each other on, is a wonderful sight. Over the years he has developed a tremendous understanding with a horse I have the privilege of knowing, Jazzie, and she is more than happy to play along with him. In fact they've become great friends.

The point I'm making is that dogs (all animals for that matter) have common needs which affect all of them and they have individual needs as well. If you are going to be fair to your companions, and make them happy and contented, you have to be able to satisfy both needs (well, obviously within reason).

Never underestimate animals. They are not simpler versions of humans in furry or feathery coats but complicated creatures. Dogs, for instance, naturally live in packs but they are not equals within the pack. There will be a strict hierarchy and each dog will either naturally assume its place or fight to establish it, usually in a short, sharp fight that is quickly over with little damage done.

Once established, the leader will expect to be first through doors, first into the car, to lead the walk and even be fed first. By recognising that fact you help to reinforce the pack order and that means more contented animals. Once the order is clear there is no more fighting and even the sounds of raised voices in the family can cause concern in dogs because it threatens the pack's unity. Heaven knows why, but they see humans as part of the pack and yet somehow separate in terms of leadership. A dog which knows he is the alpha male and leader amongst other dogs will surrender that role when dealing with you.

It's easy for all of us to criticise others about the way they treat animals but we have to be 100 per cent sure that we're being fair ourselves.

How often have you seen a grossly overweight dog who no longer runs like the wind or bounds with energy? A fat dog is likely to suffer from arthritis and die younger but the owner would probably say they loved their animal dearly and be shocked to be called cruel.

Leaving dogs on their own all day is another frequent problem. As we've seen, dogs are pack animals and must have company to be happy. On their own, they'll be lonely and at the end of the day be in distress because they'll need to relieve themselves. Once a dog is house-trained, they'll be very upset if they foul the house. Would the person who expects his or her dog to hold it in all day be comfortable not going to the loo for 10 or 11 hours? If your house is empty all day, it's not fair to keep a dog.

While dogs need to be dogs they can sometimes behave in a way that we would probably claim is very human. In his book, *Dogs Never Lie About Love* (available from Viva!), Jeffrey Masson tells a very touching story. It's about a Cornish man who lost his mongrel terrier in a part of Cornwall that is littered with old, disused tin-mine shafts. He assumed, sadly, that his dog had fallen down one of the shafts and was probably dead.

The lost dog had a friend, a little female fox terrier, and the two of them had been in the habit of wandering across the moors together. The man noticed that the fox terrier still went out onto the moors but always in the same direction. He followed her and she led him to an old mine shaft and from deep down inside he could distinctly hear barking.

A rescue party found the little mongrel about 40 feet down and with him were scraps of bread and the bone from a joint of meat which the man recognised as his last

Sunday's dinner. The fox terrier had quite clearly been helping to keep her friend alive.

Another big issue for dogs is exercise. Can you give enough? Dogs must be exercised for their mental and physical health. Large breeds need at least 16 km (10 miles) a day; medium breeds such as Labradors need 9 km (6 miles); and small pooches at least 3-4 km (2-3 miles). *You* don't have to cover that distance – your dog will run around more than you and you could throw a ball.

You must train your dog to be able to go off the lead. It is essential that she is taken for walks in places where she can have freedom. If a dog is never allowed to have a good run and explore, she'll soon become frustrated and unhappy. Remember, unlike humans, dogs always want their walk, no matter what the weather!

Top cat

Cats are equally complex but in different ways. I have studied domestic and feral cats – domesticated cats that have been forced to live wild, usually forming colonies – and they are all individuals. People are too eager to stereotype cats and describe them as loners, as if they were all the same. They aren't, in fact they are as individual as humans. Some are extremely sociable and will visit cats in other colonies and are quite clearly saying hello. Others will never leave their own colony. Some are extremely popular and gregarious, others are clearly not liked as much, and some are quite solitary. And of course there is always a top cat. All these factors are part of a cat's daily routine and the different interactions are important elements of their lives.

Much the same kind of interactions go on with

domesticated cats when they are out and about in gardens. There will be battles over sex (though cats should be neutered) and over territory. Their lives are governed by complex unwritten rules so, remarkably, they even have joint areas such as neutral alleys where, by mutual consent, no fighting takes place. When studying ethology, I watched and followed feral and domestic cats for weeks. Many explore the outside world every day with obvious interest and even relish. When they have the opportunity, such as in open countryside, the females explore an area of six acres and the males about seventeen.

Deny a cat this ability to interact, to develop and use his senses and instincts, and you deny him a fundamental part of who and what he is. Some cats, of course, don't want to go out and that of course is also fine. When I had to keep my own big tabby, called Teatime, in for a week, he was fine for two or three days and then began to go 'stir-crazy'. He would lie in hiding and when I opened the door he would fly for the opening and compete with me to get out.

There are differences between countries and in the US it is much more risky to allow cats out. They face threats of being killed as pests, captured for vivisection, abused by sick idiots or hit by traffic. But these risks are not the same everywhere. I believe you have to assess the risks – just as you do with children when deciding when to allow them to go out alone or ride a bike – and weigh the risks against the needs of the cat. If the dangers are so great in allowing a cat freedom or you can't provide extensive outside runs, then you should seriously consider whether it is right to keep a cat at all.

Unfortunately, there are now so many cats – at seven million they are the most popular companion animal in Britain – that they have become a serious threat to many species of small wildlife such as songbirds, voles, shrews and field mice. To reduce the damage and the number of abandoned kitties, it's vital that everyone neuters their cats (and the same goes for other animal friends).

Horse sense

Horses are another animal subjected to a great deal of abuse, mostly through sheer ignorance or neglect. Never kid yourself that a horse is now a tamed and entirely domesticated animal. Far from it, horses have all their natural wild instincts coursing through their bodies and left to their own devices would probably do quite well without humans.

Humans have bred huge horses such as the Shire to carry armoured knights into battle. Clydesdales were bred for a life of labour – dragging coal wagons day after day from the Scottish coal mines. Others have been bred for speed and are abused in entirely different ways in horse racing. As I was writing this chapter, four horses were destroyed in one single race at Aintree in Liverpool, where they ran the Grand National.

Eight thousand thoroughbred foals are born in Britain each year but less than half make it to the racecourse. The 'failures' end up at the abattoir. Life for those that make it to the racetrack is not a bed of roses. Horses are often run at two years old, before their bones have matured, making them prone to injury. Gruelling year-round racing and hard tracks lead to 250 deaths in UK racetracks every year. (Imagine the outcry if just one human athlete always died when racing in the Olympics.) A further 3000 horses drop out each year due to injuries or exhaustion, and veterinary reports reveal that a staggering 100 per cent of horses that race have stomach ulcers and up to three quarters haemorrhage into their lungs. Most worn-out racehorses are slaughtered. Horse racing journalist Bill Finley says, 'The thoroughbred racehorse is a genetic mistake. It runs too fast, its frame is too large, and its legs are far too small. As long as mankind demands that it run at high speeds under stressful conditions, horses will die at racetracks.' The awful truth is that as soon as money is made out of animals, they become disposable objects.

But it isn't just racehorses who suffer. For example, how often have you seen a horse on her own in a field? This is one of the worst things you can do to her. Horses are herd animals and their survival and safety depends on the herd. They have evolved strong social habits and interact with each other. Sometimes they will thunder around a field together leaping into the air and bucking, covering the area with such speed and power that they seem almost to fill it. Other times they will stand quietly, two horses together, mutually grooming each other, each nibbling the other's back, their eyes dreamy with ecstasy. Put a horse in a field on her own and she can do none of these important social things and she will fear for her own safety because there is no one to warn her of coming danger – it might only be a plastic bag floating by but to the horse it may be a leopard.

Because a solitary horse appears to show no concern doesn't mean a thing. She may have worn herself out whinnying for company for years and now is resigned that no friend is ever going to arrive. And almost certainly, deep inside, is that hollow stress of fear and a sense of isolation.

Pity polly

A parrot or budgie alone in a cage is a familiar sight. But these are social birds whose natural homes are the semi-tropical lands or rainforests where they fly at incredible speeds, often in large flocks calling and shouting raucously to each other. They should never be condemned to solitary confinement. I think it is highly questionable whether they should be kept at all. The usual excuse is that they are bred in captivity, as though a couple of generations of breeding from captive birds has eliminated all their wild instincts. What nonsense. Perhaps the biggest danger is that a 'legit-imate' bird trade provides all kinds of loopholes for the 'ille-gitimate' bird trade. With false documents or mixed cargoes, wild caught birds still flood the market.

This trade in beautiful wild birds is decimating wild flocks and condemning unknowing little creatures to a short and miserable life full of stress and incomprehension. They require very special treatment and foods, and their environment, by comparison with their native homes from which they were stolen, are barren, sterile and unful-filling. It's difficult to obtain accurate figures but of the 130,000 parrots and other exotic birds imported into Britain, about 20,000 die within the first few weeks. Even those who do survive may only live for a fraction of their natural lifespan. Parrots are likely to live no longer than about five years, when their natural life expectancy is about 50 years. It's much the same for smaller birds.

They are caught in the wild by various cruel methods:

taken from their nests before they are able to fly; driven into almost invisible 'mist' nets; or by having a sticky substance spread on the branches where they perch – they are unable to tear their feet out of it and the poachers simply come along and drag them out of the tree.

They are often wrapped up and hidden inside other merchandise when they are smuggled into western countries and sometimes have to endure days without food or water. Of course many don't survive. Others are crammed into overcrowded crates with hundreds of other birds of different species. That forced closeness between alien birds is itself highly stressful. It's estimated that for every living bird that arrives in a foreign country, a further four have died, either through rough handling when captured, shock from the ordeal or through thirst or heat stress during the crating and transport. This means that nearly 400,000 beautiful birds die every year simply to satisfy some British people's desire to keep a pretty bird in a cage. Similar death rates are happening in all western and developed countries and so the final toll runs into tens of millions. It is forcing many species of bird to the point of extinction.

Personally, I find it extremely painful to have to watch any little creature in a cage but particularly a bird. From time immemorial humans have watched birds as they soared on the wing, the world spread out beneath them. It has so inspired us with a desire to be as free as them that every child imagines and dreams about being able to fly. And what do we do? We imprison birds in tiny cages and then pretend they like it that way. I would love to see every bird-cage manufacturer in the world go out of business and I would shed not a single tear.

Fish have feelings too

This sad story of exploitation and destruction is almost the same for exotic fish. These wonderfully colourful creatures are big business. They, too, are caught in the wild some-times in unimaginably damaging ways. They are often forced out of their hiding places in coral reefs by divers who carry washing-up bottles filled with dilute solutions of poison such as strychnine and puff it into the cracks and crevices in the coral. The effect on the fish is to shock it so severely that it loses control and drifts out from its hiding place almost unconscious. It is then grabbed and bagged and most never survive the ordeal. The impact on coral reefs is so severe it is destroying them and all the other creatures that depend upon these rich ecosystems. Those who do survive often look forward to a life in a barren and sterile aquarium where they can swim from one end to the other in a second or two. Like all crea-tures, fish have complicated interactions in their natural world and this is taken away from them. I would like to see aquarium manufacturers join the bird-cage manufac-turers on the unemployment register.

Hutch horror

Many other companion animals are denied a fulfilling life, often through ignorance. Rabbits are a good exam-ple. Far too many are kept in tiny hutches – it's like *Cell Block H*, with H for hutch! Often they're not given the room to exercise properly and, as sociable animals, many are kept alone. Rabbits should be kept in pairs that get on with each other or compatible family groups.

A Viva! supporter noticed that one of her neighbours kept two rabbits together in a tiny hutch and they were never let out. She persuaded the neighbour to let her have them and she immediately liberated them, giving them the run of her house and garden. She made a horrifying discovery – they hated each other. They hated with such a venom that she could not allow them in the same part of the house together and when they went outside they had to do so separately. Just imagine it – they were cooped up together in just a few square feet for over 18 months. What hell that must have been! The lesson is, never assume two animals will get on together – particularly two male rabbits – and always find out about an animal's behaviour, its needs and habits.

Many people harm their animal companions through ignorance. They don't take the trouble to find out what their animal needs. It's common for people to buy an exotic species and feed it the wrong diet – for example, giving a vegetarian lizard a diet of meat and then wondering why she has become ill!

All animals are individuals and deserve respect yet so often they are expected to fit into our plans. How often do you see people tugging on dogs' leads, making them choke, if they want to sniff something? Some people even stop their dog from ever smelling or playing with other dogs. Imagine the result if we stopped a child from exploring her world!

If you decide to keep an animal, the best way to help reduce the number of strays is to go to your animal rescue shelter. Don't buy an animal – it encourages cruelty and exploitation. Go to your library and loan books on whatever type of animal you decide on. Find out everything about their needs: shelter; diet; whether they can be kept on their own, like cats, or must be with their own kind, like mice, horses and us! Like charity, action for animals begins at home!

Success Stories

- Puppy farms – where female dogs were forced to have litter after litter, their pups taken away too young and sold – were banned in Britain in 2000. Several animal rights groups worked to introduce a law which stops commercial breeders from making a bitch have more than six litters and from making her have a litter within a year of the last. Breeders now have to have a licence to sell puppies and be inspected annually by a vet.
- The World Society for the Protection of Animals have established a rehabilitation centre – the Centro Rehabilitation – in Colombia, Central America. Its primary purpose is to provide a shelter where confiscated rare and endangered birds and other animals can be received, treated and returned to the wild. Already hundreds of birds have been saved by the Centre and the hope is eventually to build a string of centres around the world.

Action for Animals

- Neuter your companion animal – with animal populations spiralling out of control, this is an essential and responsible action. An unneutered cat can be responsible for 20,000 kittens in his lifetime!
- Adopt your animal from a rescue centre (listed in *Yellow Pages* under Animal Welfare Societies). This will ensure you're not supporting greedy, cruel breeders and you may be saving a beautiful, innocent creature from being put to death.
- Don't buy exotic animals. For example, tortoises are

rarely bred in captivity – most are taken from the wild and die either in transit or within a year of them arriving here.

- Don't cage a bird – they're meant to be free and, no matter how much you try, you can't recreate their natural home where they belong. Many birds are captured in the wild and die *en route* to their destination.

- Liberate goldfish! Bowls mean a life of boredom and stress for goldfish. It's as bad as keeping hens in battery cages. Goldfish are shoal animals and need companions. They also need space, natural plants, and places to hide or they will feel vulnerable and anxious. If you know anyone who keeps their fish like this, try to persuade them either to buy a big oxygenated tank with lots of real plants and hidey holes and some chums or release the fish into a village pond or friend's garden pond (contact Viva! for more info).

- Boycott pet shops that sell animals and tell them why.

- Microchip your cat or dog so they can be traced if they are lost or injured.

- Support Animal Aid's campaign against DIY chains that sell animals – such as small mammals, fish and birds, plus exotic species like lizards, snakes and spiders – in their stores.

- Support the World Parrot Trust and the WSPA to end the trade in wild birds.

- Support the People's Dispensary for Sick Animals (PDSA) – they give free vet treatment to 1.4 million animals of disadvantaged owners each year. Contact them for a Challenge Pack which gives young people lots of fun tasks to help the charity. Rummage through your clothes and bric-a-brac to see what you can donate to one of the PDSA's charity shops – there are 120 in the UK.

- The oldest cat rescue charity in Britain is the Cats Protection League – contact them if you want to adopt an abandoned kitty and for info on how to care for her.
- Support Hillside Animal Sanctuary's campaign against horseracing and adopt one of the ex-racehorses they have rescued.
- Write to your MP (phone 020 7219 4272 for their name) at the House of Commons, London SW1A 0AA to call for a review of racehorse welfare.

If You See Cruelty

It is a horrible feeling to discover that a neighbour or someone you know is mistreating an animal, but you can help. If it's a matter of simple education, you or your parents could try talking to the owner. If that doesn't work, or you don't want to take that route, call the RSPCA. It's their job to send out inspectors in all cases of suspected cruelty and they should be glad to have a caring member of the public call them. Call their 24-hour-a-day cruelty line on 0870 55 55 999, or the police. Have the following information ready:

- A description of the animal(s) involved.
- The precise location of the animal(s).
- The names and addresses of other witnesses.
- The registration number of any vehicle involved.
- The name and address of the suspect(s) if known.

The RSPCA should not give your name to the animal's owner.

The RSPCA do not come out for stray animals. If you find one, try giving her food and water. If the animal isn't too frightened to be approached, call or take him to a local animal rescue centre that does not kill healthy animals.

'Animals are dependent on us, trusting as a child. They are a responsibility we have no right to neglect, nor to violate by cruelty.'
James Herriot

'The love for all living creatures is the most noble attribute of humans.'
Charles Darwin

'What I have always loved about dogs is how directly and intensely they express emotions. Every time I told my cocker spaniel, Taffy, that we were going for a walk, she would launch into a celebratory dance which ended with her racing around the room – her joy could not be contained... hardly any creature can express pure joy so vividly as a dog.'
Jeffrey Masson, author of *Dogs Never Lie About Love* and *When Elephants Weep*

Chapter 7

Animal Farm

The Life of Farmed Animals

Jody Meeson, 15, of Lincoln, had loved animals for as long as she could remember. Her bedroom walls were covered in pictures of lions and tigers, cats and dogs – and pigs. If anyone had suggested she should eat a lion she would have thought them mad. But eating pigs? Jody hadn't even thought about it.

'My Dad was a terrible joker. I can remember even when I was quite little, driving through the countryside and seeing new-born lambs in a field. They were so gorgeous and cuddly and I said I'd like to take one home. My dad said he'd like one, too – so he could have roast lamb and mint sauce! It was disgusting and the more I told him so, the more he laughed. But I ate roast lamb as well and so deep down I knew he was probably more honest than me. My way of coping with it was not to think about it.

'It was the same with pigs. I've always loved them, yet I used to eat bacon sarnies and ham pizza. But there came a day when I had to face up to the fact that I was a bit of a hypocrite.

'A friend of mine, Sam, was doing a project on sausages for food tech. and had managed to blag her way into visiting a pig farm. Because I like pigs, I decided to tag along for the ride. There was a little part of me that was nervous because I knew I was going to see animals that would eventually be killed and eaten – maybe even by me. But I went anyway. I don't really know what I was expecting to see, probably pigs snuffling around a farmyard – but it wasn't anything like that.

'We started at the very beginning – the birth. There was no friendly pigsty and mounds of straw with a contented mum nuzzling her piglets. Not a bit of it. There was a huge shed with a few grimy, cobwebbed windows. It was a shed that looked like it should house a garage or a small factory. The inside was divided by metal tubes into separate stalls and in most of them was a huge mother pig, a sow.

'All the pigs were lying down in stalls not much longer or wider than their bodies. They looked completely dejected. The floor was made of concrete and wooden slats which were covered with urine and poo and there wasn't a blade of grass or a strand of straw to be seen. In effect, the poor creatures could barely stand up, couldn't turn round and I couldn't for the life of me work out why.

'And then I was told. These were farrowing crates, where the sows are sent to give birth and they spend about a month like this, before being made pregnant again only a few days after their piglets are taken away.

'A pig near to me had just given birth and had a litter of tiny little piglets – about ten of them. They could reach their mother through the metal bars in order to suckle milk from her but the mother couldn't reach her piglets. She just had to lie there like a beached whale, acting as nothing more than a milk machine. The metal bars were necessary, I was told, to stop the sow rolling on her piglets and killing them. I wasn't convinced – I bet that pigs in the wild don't accidentally kill their young.

'There were dozens of sows in the shed, all of them held in these metal barred prisons and I found the whole idea appalling. But not as appalling as the sight I saw in some of the stalls. Lying alongside the little living piglets were some dead ones. They had been there so long that they were turning black and stank to high heaven. Flies were buzzing around everywhere.

'I was horrified and pointed it out to the lad who was showing us around. He just laughed and said someone would clear them out later. I'd seen all I wanted to and went back outside to wait for Sam. I was genuinely shocked, probably more than I've ever been in my life. I couldn't believe it was legal to treat animals like that with so little care or feeling. And I couldn't believe that people could work there and simply close their eyes to the suffering. It seemed inhuman to me.

'Of course, I'm vegetarian now. When I drive through the countryside and see all the big, ugly sheds that seem to be on most farms, I dread to think what's going on inside them.'

Welcome to the wonderful world of modern meat production. What Jody witnessed was a typical example of factory farming. Humans claim to be intelligent creatures but what they do to animals is neither intelligent nor kind.

Just imagine for a minute that you're a Martian. You've landed on planet Earth and you want to find out more about what humans eat. Through a bit of scientific research before arriving, you know that eating meat, fish and dairy products causes heart disease, cancer and a string of other diseases such as diabetes, kidney stones and food poisoning.

You also know that livestock farming is a hopelessly inefficient way of feeding people, that it causes pollution and environmental destruction on a staggering scale. Having an average dollop of common sense, you'd expect to find that most people on Earth would be vegetarians or vegans.

Imagine the surprise when you discover that every year in Britain alone, almost 900 million animals are slaughtered and eaten – 2.4 million killed every day – and that the average Briton scoffs their own weight in meat every year. In the US, in 1999, 9734 million animals were killed for food, and worldwide a mind–boggling 43.2 billion.

You quickly learn that humans spend a lot of time telling everyone how caring they are and how much they love animals. You see that lots of magazines carry pictures of cuddly little animals and on TV you see a whole load of programmes about how sick animals are made better by caring people and how their owners are extremely sad if their furry friends die.

So, just as it did for Jody, the real shock would come when you then looked at how the food animals that most people eat are kept. You would shake your head in disbelief and you would probably ask a very obvious question: 'Why do you treat some animals so well and other animals so badly?'

You would probably find it hard to understand when these same people replied that all animals, including food animals, are kept well and to the very highest standards of welfare. They usually make it sound like a Butlin's holiday camp. You would then be forced to ask whether these people had ever actually seen how food animals are kept.

And you would almost certainly get the answer 'no'.

So how are animals treated down on the farm? First it's important to remember that all farmed animals have been bred from wild animals and they retain their instincts and needs. Cattle, sheep, pigs and chickens were domesticated about 10,000 years ago and were kept outdoors. The number of animals farmed for food was tiny in comparison to today. Humans evolved from vegetarian apes and, in fact, the diet of most people was very low in meat until the last century when meat production increased dramatically. In Britain, in 1946, 2 million cattle, 7 milllion sheep, 2 million pigs and 40 million chickens were slaughtered. In 1999 numbers had skyrocketed to 2.3 million cattle, 9 million sheep, 16 million pigs and 800 million chickens.

This is because after World War II things began to change. Farmers were encouraged to produce as much meat as possible and they found they could grow more animals if they kept them in sheds and took the food to them. It was mostly chickens and pigs that were first treated like this in the UK but in other countries, such as the US, cattle were farmed in this way as well.

No one seemed to care much about what cramming so many animals together might do to them. They were unable to live naturally. They couldn't run or even walk very far. There was no grass or grazing, just filthy straw covered with their own faeces. Even the food was unnatural.

None of this would have been possible without new powerful drugs such as antibiotics, discovered just after the War. Without them animals could never have been kept in these cramped conditions since diseases would have spread rapidly from one to another.

Before long, the producers discovered that not only were antibiotics good for stopping diseases but they were excellent for making the animals grow faster. So, for many animals, they were given drugs every day of their lives, usually mixed in with their feed.

Of course, they should have known there would be a price to pay for treating animals in this way. The animals were miserably unhappy, lived a short and horrible life, and were unhealthy. Their meat contained food-poisoning bacteria such as E. coli, salmonella and campylobacter and traces of antibiotics. The bacteria these drugs were designed to kill evolved and found a way of surviving. The outcome was 'superbugs' – bugs that can kill humans and which it is almost impossible for us to treat. For example, a strain of food poisoning salmonella (called salmonella DT-104) found in pork, sausages, chicken and meat paste is resistant to most antibiotics, including the fluoro-quinolones – an important class of drugs used to treat diseases in people. One quarter of human salmonella infections are now resistant to drug therapy.

For years – many, many years – people who really cared about animals kept telling farmers and govern-ments that it was wrong to treat animals like this. But they were ignored and increasing numbers of farmers were encouraged to rear their animals this way. And it's still going on. You don't have to be a Martian to think that the whole thing is crazy and cruel.

Piggies' plight

Pigs are among the most intelligent of animals and are closer to a chimpanzee than a dog in intelligence. They lived wild in Britain's woods until they were hunted to extinction in the seventeenth century. They fed on seeds, nuts (particularly beech nuts), insects, roots and sometimes small mammals. Their snouts and strong necks helped them to grub in the forest floor unearthing tasty morsels. Not keen on temperature changes, they would find shade under the trees in the summer and make nests from forest litter – twigs, leaves, branches, dried ferns – in which to have their young and to keep out the winter chill. The piglets would suckle from their mother for up to three months.

Modern farm pigs are still closely related to their wild cousins but, because of my work with Viva! filming numerous British pig farms, I can tell you their life is very different. There are about 800,000 breeding sows in Britain – the kind that Jody saw – and about two thirds of them live under what is politely called 'intensive conditions'. This means a shared concrete pen a few feet square and it's here that the sows spend their pregnancy. There is usually nothing to do, nowhere to go, nothing to see in the dimmest of light – just endless boredom.

But even this is an advance on what happened in the UK until 1998. Sows were held in metal-barred stalls called 'dry sow stalls', which were just a few inches wider than the sows' bodies. The pigs were unable to take more than one pace forward and one pace back and could only lie down with difficulty. As if this wasn't bad enough, these intelligent creatures were sometimes fitted with a collar around their middle or neck, which was then chained to the floor. They had become nothing more than piglet bearing machines.

Unsurprisingly, many of them showed what's called 'stereotypic behaviour' where they would repeat the same action over and over again. In other words they had gone mad from the terrible boredom and frustration. Although this barbaric system is now outlawed in Britain, sow stalls are still common all over Europe, the US and Australia and are spreading to the rest of the world.

When the time for the sow to give birth gets close, she is moved from the pen to a farrowing crate. It is here she gives birth – no nest, no comforts, none of the pride and contentment that all animals show when they have babies. No thought at all is given to her needs. She has become a unit of production exactly as if she were a tin of peas or a stereo.

The piglets are removed from their mother at only three weeks old – far too young to leave her and far too young to start eating solid foods, but it happens anyway. The piglets develop stomach upsets since their digestive system can't cope with non-milk food and so this is when the antibiotic treatments begin.

Life for them is no better than for their mothers and their first 'home' is often a 'flat-deck system'. This is exactly what it sounds like – bare, perforated metal floors like the deck of a ship, with walls to match. Dozens of little animals are imprisoned with no straw, no hay, no toys and nothing to do. Often the lights are kept extremely dim or are switched off altogether for the first month of their lives.

What do you think you would do in these circumstances? You would become extremely unhappy, frustrated and bored and you'd probably pick fights because your life was so unnatural. Of course, that's exactly what happens and to try to prevent the piglets from damaging each other, their main teeth and the ends of their tails are cut off (usually without anaesthetic) when they are just one week old. And you thought it was bad going to the dentist!

The cure for aggression doesn't have to be mutilation. Piglets that live outside, who run on grass and explore trees and bushes, and root in the ground don't bite each other. Obviously, the answer is to allow them to live naturally. But, of course, that costs too much in today's farming world, where profit is everything.

More than 90 per cent of piglets killed for meat are factory farmed in this way. In investigations of farms all over Britain, Viva! exposed diseased, dead and dying animals. In almost every fattening unit there was glaring neglect and indifference – broken legs, abscesses, ruptured stomachs, animals coughing with pneumonia, others panting from meningitis, cuts and lacerations from the perforated metal on which they are forced to live.

One farm I investigated in Yorkshire, which supplied major supermarkets, looked almost derelict, with junk and debris everywhere and only an array of grimy windowless sheds as the giveaway to what it farmed.

There was no light inside but a cacophony of noise – a scrambling and clattering of animals in fear. The camera lights revealed baby pigs in barren metal pens and the noise was their feet on the bare metal floors as they charged to get away. One pig had a broken leg, others were stunted with a wasting disease from which they will almost certainly die. Some were lame, others had deformed spines. Outside in a rusting trailer was a pile of rotting corpses, discoloured and bloated from days of decay, half submerged in putrid rainwater.

As they grow bigger all pigs are moved to bigger pens

but even when they're fully grown, weighing about 100 kg, they may be allowed no more than half a square metre of space – that's 200 big pigs in a space just 10 metres by 10 metres. And this is legal. In another of the farms I visited, there were around 200 large pigs in an area of about 10 metres by 12 metres. The pigs squealed and screamed, biting in their desperation to be let out.

Pigs have been made to grow so fast that they are killed at five or six months when they are still really babies. Their flesh is used for bacon, ham, pepperoni, sausages, pork chops and joints. If allowed, they would live for 20 years or more.

Fowl deeds

The other animals that are now almost entirely factory farmed are chickens and 800 million of them are killed in Britain every year. They are kept in sheds called 'broiler houses', as many as 60,000 in one shed. Each bird is allowed just the space of a computer screen.

The concrete floor is covered with sawdust, wood shavings or straw but it soon becomes soaked with the birds' excrement. The filth may attract flies and other insects that spread disease. This is how nearly all chickens live for their short, six-week life.

They spend the time standing in their own filth and can be in terrible pain from 'hock' burns – burns on their feet and legs or even their breasts from the ammonia in their droppings. Just imagine what a small mouth ulcer feels like and then multiply it several times.

The windowless sheds are artificially lit for 23 hours out of 24 to prevent the chicks from sleeping because when they're not sleeping they're eating and putting on weight. A bird that fattens quickly means more money and profit is the whole point of modern farming.

The birds are killed when they weigh about 1.8 kg at only six weeks old. They go to their deaths with the bodies of adult birds but the blue eyes and the high-pitched cheep of little chicks.

As with pigs, antibiotics are essential and are fed to all broiler chickens every day of their lives. They make them grow so fast that their bones often don't develop properly and break under their ballooning weight. Eight out of ten chickens have broken bones, deformed feet or legs and other defects to their skeletons.

Often their hearts are not big enough to pump suffi-cient blood to their oversized bodies and as a result, birds that are still babies die from heart disease. About 40 million die in the sheds every year.

When you look inside a broiler shed just after the day-old chicks have been put there, it doesn't look too bad. At least there's some room for these beautiful little crea-tures to run around on the dry straw and wood shavings. Look again after nearly five weeks and it's a different sight. The little balls of fluff have transformed into big, heavy, white-feathered chickens and they have expanded to fill the entire space. The dry floor has become soaked and sodden with droppings and the stench is breathtak-ing – literally. The ammonia from their droppings can burn your eyes and cause you to gasp for breath.

Every six weeks, the catchers come into the sheds and cram the birds into crates to be transported to the slaugh-terhouse. Only then is the floor cleaned out and new litter laid for the next batch of birds.

Chickens are also descended from a wild creature – the

red jungle fowl of India – but the life of a jungle fowl and a chicken are devastatingly different.

Little by little, people who fight for animal welfare have managed to get small improvements but the farmers and governments resist every suggestion until so many people complain that eventually they feel they have to make changes. Without pressure from those who care about animals, it's likely that nothing would ever change.

So is the answer to eat turkey instead? No, I don't think so! When you see a turkey flying free in its natural environment, their wing and tail feathers shimmering red-green and copper, contrasting with their white wing bars, it makes you shudder to think about those that have been bred for food. These poor white monstrosities can barely walk let alone fly. Their semi-wild nature makes life in the factory farm sheds very stressful indeed.

It's always seemed really strange to me that in Britain we celebrate Christmas – supposedly a time of goodwill, friendliness and peace on earth – by cutting the throats of nearly 20 million turkeys, 10 million ducks and an assortment of other birds.

Modern farming is a major con. The only animals you ever see are those that are allowed to roam around freely in the fields. These are only the tip of the iceberg and the vast majority of animals you never see because they're hidden away in sheds.

The low life of a battery
Chickens that are bred for their eggs have, if possible, an even worse time. If you've ever watched a hen you'll know that she struts around endlessly during daylight, searching in the grass for grubs and seeds, kicking the

earth aside with her powerful legs. She loves nothing better than to dust bathe, fluffing the grit over all her feathers. When she thinks there might be food around she can run like crazy, her legs stretching out, her body waddling from side to side.

Who could possibly look at these restless, harmless creatures and decide to cram five of them into a cage little bigger than a microwave oven and keep them there for their entire lives? Unfortunately someone did and today 80 per cent of all the eggs eaten in Britain come from these cruel battery-cage systems.

Of course the producers don't advertise the fact – in fact they try to hide it by packaging the eggs in boxes saying 'country fresh' or some other misleading claim. What they don't say is that their eggs come from chickens who can never scratch in the ground, never perch, never run nor even walk.

Just consider this! A chicken's wing span is 76 cm and the width of the cage in which she is forced to live is 50 cm. Not even one bird can stretch her wings let alone five. Sometimes the cages look as though they go on forever, row upon row stacked up on top of each other. In older types of sheds, the birds' faeces drop through the cages to a pit below where it stays for the short two-year lifespan the birds are allowed. Again, the stench can be overwhelming. We can walk away from it, the birds can't.

The hens never see daylight because they live a completely unnatural life governed by artificial lighting. It is kept on for 17 hours a day to fool the birds into laying more eggs. Birds that in the wild would lay only about 20 eggs a year lay an incredible 300 in the sheds due to intensive light, selective breeding and high-protein food.

The result is, of course, a disaster for the birds. This trickery, together with lack of fresh air, lack of exercise and overcrowding, has led to a string of diseases and the bones of battery hens are often so brittle that they snap like dry twigs. About one third have broken bones.

The University of Edinburgh reviewed all the scientific studies on battery hens and came to the conclusion that 'they suffer'. You really didn't need a scientist to tell you that. The two million UK battery hens that die from their living conditions every year are evidence enough I would have thought.

The producers' (you can't really call them farmers) answer is that only happy hens lay eggs. It's like saying that only happy people poo. Laying eggs is a bodily function over which the hens have no control.

What we do know is that laying eggs is a very private affair for a hen and she desperately wants to be on her own to do it. Fat chance in a tiny cage, so she often struggles to hide beneath her cage mates. As soon as she's laid her egg it rolls away across the sloping wire floor and onto a conveyor belt where it is carried to the packing station.

When all a bird's natural instincts are so badly frustrated, the outcome is always the same – aggression. Just as with pigs, the producers have a brutal way of trying to stop birds pecking each other. When the chicks are just a few days old, the ends of their beaks are sliced off with a red hot blade. Some die from bleeding or shock and it's thought that many feel the pain of amputation throughout their entire lives.

So the answer is to eat free-range eggs, I can almost hear you thinking. Well, as with so many things in life, the answer is not that simple. Cramming thousands of birds into a single shed, providing them with a few 'pop holes' (openings to the outside world) and calling this 'free range' is a bit of a con. Unfortunately it's how most free-range hens are reared.

Most of the birds can't even get outside because they're terrified of crossing so many other birds. Cannibalism, aggression and injuries are all rife and so the same old cruel practice of beak trimming is still too often used.

If you want to eat eggs, there is one scheme in the UK which guarantees they are from hens that are truly free range. It is run by the Soil Association and ensures that *all* the chickens can strut around outside when they please; eat natural, varied food; dust bathe and do all the things hens want to do. Look out for egg boxes stamped with the Soil Association's approval.

But there is a hidden side to egg production (even for the Soil Association's eggs) that no one ever talks about, and it's the little male chicks. Unlike chickens to be eaten, egg-laying chickens are bred to put on as little weight as possible – well, weight costs money – and lay as many eggs as possible. Of course, males can't lay eggs but they're also too scrawny for meat. At one day old the little chicks are sexed and the males are placed on a special conveyor belt. It takes them nowhere but a big plastic bin.

They cascade into it, piling on top of each other, with the ones at the bottom struggling for air and often suffocating to death. The bins full of these little yellow balls of fluff are transferred to a gas chamber where they are killed with CO_2 gas – 40 million of them every year. It's exactly the same for all male chicks whether born in a battery or free-range system.

Ducks out of water

No doubt like me you've spent many happy days feeding ducks on your local river or pond. To state the obvious, ducks are waterbirds – evolved to eat, swim, dive, clean themselves and play in water. Yet an investigation by Viva! has revealed that even these creatures are factory farmed and placed in an environment where they never even see water, except in their drinkers. Denied this fundamental requirement, they can't preen properly and find it hard to keep warm. Without water they may develop eye problems and even blindness. Without water, their lives have little meaning.

Although white, most farmed ducks are descended from Mallards – the brown ducks and handsome, green-headed drakes seen on every village pond. Like them, the farmed ducks would love to fly at 50 mph, to choose a mate and to live for 15 years or more. Fly? Some can hardly walk because of leg deformities. There's no mating and life ends brutally after seven weeks. As you'll see in the next chapter, many will be fully conscious when their throats are cut.

All across the world, Britain included, ducks are being driven off ponds and into intensive sheds. A staggering 90 per cent of duck meat sold in restaurants and supermarkets is from birds reared indoors. This involves up to 10,000 ducks caged in one 'unit', with faeces-sodden litter that can result in painful ammonia burns. In the crowded sheds there's no sun, no wind and no rain to run off their backs, just constant, artificial light. Unsurprisingly, many become diseased and die. Others are pushed on to their backs where, unable to right themselves, they starve to death.

A duck eats by straining plankton and tasty morsels from the water through its beak. This vital organ is as sensitive as a fingertip. Despite this, Viva! has exposed the fact that one producer, Kerry Foods, slices the ends off the Barbary duck's beak to prevent 'feather pulling' – a product of the stressful conditions! The mutilation can lead to constant pain.

A UK-based company, Cherry Valley, is the biggest producer of duck meat in the world, describing itself as 'an enterprise which is both the biggest and most intensive of its kind anywhere... as many as 85,000 birds can be looked after by only one person' (Cherry Valley Farms' promotional booklet).

Beautiful birds, still driven by a powerful call of the wild are still being denied all freedom in factory farms while those responsible boast about it.

Poor bleaters

OK, I hear you say, at least the animals we do see in the fields have a good life. If only! Take sheep. They are reared for their wool, skin, meat and sometimes milk. At least 'free range' does mean free range for most of them. They live in the open with their own kind, eat a natural diet and when they are babies they are looked after and nurtured by their own mothers – something that's denied to almost all factory farmed animals.

But of course it isn't as simple as that. Having watched huntsmen maraud across the British countryside on the pretence of protecting sheep from foxes, you'd think these animals were very special indeed. But the truth is, as explained in Chapter 2, foxes kill very few lambs – too few to be of any importance, according to the Government. Farmers, on the other hand, kill an awful lot – in the region of four million every year.

The reason is that the sheep's natural breeding cycle has been purposely interfered with to make her give birth earlier in the year. This is too early and results in death for 20 per cent of all lambs from cold, hunger, sickness or pregnancy complications.

To get pregnant by a ram, the sheep has to come into season. This is triggered by the shorter daylight hours of late autumn or winter, meaning that after five months of pregnancy she will give birth to her lamb or lambs in the early spring when the weather has started to warm up.

Many farmers, lured by the higher prices paid for early 'new season's lamb' purposely change this natural pattern to ensure the lambs are born earlier – as early as January or even December. They do it by tricking the ewe, keeping her indoors to control the amount of light and giving her hormones to fool her body. Although a sheep would usually have a single lamb, artificial insemination is now regularly making her produce two, three or even four lambs a year. Of course, she can't cope with this number which contributes to the high death rate.

The lambs are slaughtered at about four months old. The ewes are generally killed after four to eight years even though they could live to 15 or more.

Although the UK sheep industry is geared mainly to the production of lamb meat, wool also makes money. Again sheep have been carefully bred to grow more wool than nature intended. In the wild, they have an outer covering of hair with the wool making up just a fine undercoat. Today's sheep have been 'improved' to increase the wool and reduce the coarse hair.

The sheep have to be shorn every year before the weather becomes too hot and uncomfortable. It is a very stressful experience for sheep who aren't used to being handled.

Perhaps the most disgusting aspect of the wool trade is that nearly one third of all the wool used in the UK comes from slaughtered animals. Think about this next time you put on your woolly hat to keep warm.

Lose your bottle

Probably the most commonly seen farm animal in Europe is the dairy cow – usually black and white and chomping away contentedly at the grass. Well, that's what it looks like but again the truth is very different. This seemingly happy, gentle creature is probably one of the most abused farmed animals of all.

Milk is their reason for living – and it usually kills them. Surprisingly, few people seem to have any understanding of what's involved even though it's such a central part of most of our lives. Animals – all animals including humans – only give milk after they've given birth. It doesn't pour out like water from a tap but is part of the wonder of a new life and is there to feed the baby.

Dairy cows are made pregnant every year and after a nine-month pregnancy her teetering calf is taken away from her after just a day or two. That's how long it takes for the calf to suckle the essential, disease-preventing colostrum which is produced before the milk flow starts. As soon as the colostrum ceases, the calf is taken away and neither calf nor mother cow ever see each other again. This is a cruelty which would cause a national outrage if it was done to cats and dogs.

Some calves, if they look 'beefy' enough, are kept to grow into beef cattle. Most female calves are kept to replace worn out old dairy cows, such as their mothers. The real nastiness is reserved for the male, bull calves.

In most dairy-producing countries in Europe and the US, bull calves are kept for veal production. The calves are placed in solitary confinement in crates so small they can't turn round. Their feet are constantly trying to find a firm footing on the slatted wooden floors. They are fed a liquid diet so they purposely become diseased – anaemic – so that their flesh will be white. They become so desperate for solid food that they will eat their own hair. The torture ends after six months when they are slaughtered and their pale flesh served as a delicacy in expensive restaurants.

Energetic campaigning by animal rights activists in Britain won the day and veal crates were banned, the Government acknowledging they were extremely cruel. That, you would think, would be the end of the story for the UK but it wasn't. Farmers were allowed to add extra suffering to the plight of young bull calves by cramming them into lorries and transporting them across Europe to the veal crates of Spain, Italy, France and Holland.

Thousands of protesters took to the streets to try to stop the trade. They managed to reduce exports but the trade came to a complete end when the dreadful 'mad cow disease' (bovine spongiform encephalopathy or BSE for short) spread through Britain's cattle. But, having lost their export trade, some British farmers then simply took the calves from their mothers and shot them, all the time arguing for the right to send their calves to the veal crates of Europe. When farmers claim that they care about the welfare of their animals, which they do all the time, it is important not to listen to their words but to look at their deeds.

Success Stories

- The number of vegetarians has increased steadily in many parts of the world. In Britain and the USA, Viva! is a very active group campaigning against factory farming and for a vegetarian/vegan world. It has helped spur the growth to 6 million veggies (10 per cent of the UK population); and a huge 60 per cent of the UK population now reduce their meat intake. Farm Sanctuary, FARM, EarthSave, PETA, Vegan Action, Vegan Outreach, the Physicians' Committee for Responsible Medicine and the Vegetarian Resource Group in the USA, and Animal Liberation and the Vegetarian Societies in Australia have changed millions of people.
- Most large towns now have several vegetarian restaurants. Listings of them are available from animal groups. In Britain, Viva! has guides to lots of cities and towns from Brighton to Edinburgh; and the Vegan Society produces the *Vegan Travel Guide. The Vegetarian Journal's Guide to Natural Food Restaurants in the US and Canada* is also available from Viva! in the UK and the USA. In Australia, the magazine *New Vegetarian and Natural Health* does regular restaurant reviews and Sunflower Guides produce a guide to Australia and New Zealand (contact PO Box 2187, Sydney NSW 1043).

- Viva! dived into action for ducks in 2000 and got massive media coverage of the way these creatures are treated. Intrepid campaigners headed off to local supermarkets dressed as supermarket managers and ducks. The 'duck' poured a bucket of water over the 'supermarket manager' as a gesture for being totally deprived of water on the farm. It wasn't much fun for the 'supermarket managers' but the photographs in newspapers looked great and really got the message across! Within five months of launching the campaign, Harrods stopped selling factory farmed duck meat and Sainsbury's and Marks & Spencer withdrew meat from debeaked birds.

- In the European Union the battery cage will be banned in 2012. Only 'enriched' cages will be legal where the space given to hens must be increased from 450 cm^2 to 750 cm^2 and birds must be given a nest, litter, perch and scratching strip. This system is uneconomic, so it's hoped by campaigners that only free range conditions and (slightly less cruel) percheries will remain.

- A piggy victory was achieved in Britain in 1998 by Compassion in World Farming (CIWF) when the sow stall was banned. Females could no longer be kept in metal-barred stalls throughout their pregnancy.

Action for Animals

- The biggest, most powerful step you can take to end cruelty to farmed animals is to stop eating them! By going vegetarian you're saying to the world that you care about animals and they will no longer have to suffer on your behalf. Changing has never been easier

– there are literally hundreds of meat-free and fish-free products available. Contact Viva! for their guides, the *L-Plate Vegetarian* and the *L-Plate Vegan*, on what's available in shops and supermarkets; and purchase *Pam Ferris Cooks Veggie* for simple, quick recipes. Read up on nutrition and health in case you're asked lots of questions. Viva!'s *Nutrition in a Nutshell* and *The Healthiest Diet on Earth* have all the facts and will show you why the vegetarian diet is the healthiest. *The Livewire Guide to Going, Being and Staying Veggie!* tells you everything you need to know.

- 'Food for Their Future' is the name of a campaign by Viva! which reveals how eating the flesh and milk of factory farmed animals makes children ill. Help Viva! distribute leaflets for children, parents, teachers and health workers on this important issue.

- If you eat eggs, buy only those which are genuinely free range – look for the Soil Association's stamp of approval.

- Go all the way! If you have any questions about going vegan (not eating any animal products, including eggs and dairy) contact Viva! and the Vegan Society.

- CIWF and Viva! run high profile campaigns to abolish factory farming. They've had lots of successes – support them to ensure there are more.

- Write to the government's Ministry of Agriculture (MAFF) at Nobel House, 17 Smith Square, London SW1P 3JR (this department is responsible for farm-animal welfare), the Prime Minister and your MP (both at the House of Commons, London SW1A 0AA). Remember, they're only human and it was public pressure that led to the ban on veal crates and sow stalls in Britain. Contact them about any issue on farming that concerns you.

- For example, as part of Viva!'s 'Pig In Hell' campaign, your help is needed to ban the farrowing crate. A letter could go something like this:

Your name
Your address

Your MP's name (eg Ms Ima Helpful MP)
House of Commons
London SW1A 0AA

Dear MP's name (eg Ms Helpful)

I am appalled that two thirds of breeding pigs are forced to give birth in metal-barred contraptions called 'farrowing crates'. The crates are so small the animals can't walk or turn around – there is barely room to stand. However, before giving birth, females are very restless. If free, they would walk miles and build a huge nest on the forest floor of leaves and grasses. Caged in this way, sows become completely frustrated and lapse into 'stereotyped behaviour' – repeatedly attempting to build a nest on the bare hard floor on which they are trapped. In factory farms, they are rarely given even a piece of straw.

Please work to ensure that the farrowing crate is banned.

I look forward to hearing from you.

Yours sincerely
Your name

- Write to the head offices of supermarkets as well (ask Viva! for their addresses). They sell most of our food and can put huge pressure on farmers to change the way they treat animals. They also own a lot of factory farms. A letter about duck farming could read:

Your name
Your address

Chief Executive
Supermarket's name and address

Dear Chief Executive

I am shocked to discover that factory-farmed duck meat is on sale at your supermarket and I urge you to withdraw it.

In many ways, these beautiful birds are still wild animals but farmed ducks are crammed into windowless sheds. They must spend their whole lives standing on concrete floors in their own mess.

Some birds get knocked over onto their backs and cannot get up again. This must be terrifying as well as painful. With only one person looking after thousands of ducklings, sick or injured birds are left to die.

Ducks are waterbirds – without water they cannot display any of their natural behaviour. The ducks that you stock never had the chance to swim, dive, clean, play or feed in water. Without water they may suffer from poor feathers, eye problems and even blindness.

If you ever spent a Sunday afternoon feeding ducks in your local park, then you must care about these poor creatures too? Please think about what these beautiful birds had to go through and stop selling their flesh.

Thank you.

Yours sincerely
Your name

- Stand up for your beliefs! Join Viva!'s campaign to end duck farming and join in with their nationwide demonstrations outside supermarkets. It's a great opportunity for fancy dress!
- Information is power so contact: Viva! for their excellent reports on the pig, duck, ostrich and chicken industries and for their full colour guide on factory farming *Murder, She Wrote*; CIWF for reports on broiler chickens and battery hens; the Farm Animal Welfare Network for chicken, turkey and dairy info and Animal Aid for their report on sheep.
- Spread the word! Join Viva! and become a youth contact. You'll be kept in touch with all their youth campaigns against factory farming and slaughter and they'll give you step-by-step guides on how to help. Most people are shocked about the way farmed animals are treated and red-meat consumption is declining. To ensure this trend continues, Viva! needs people like you to help distribute leaflets, put up posters, invite their speakers to your school, hold demonstrations, get veggie food served at school and to contact local newspapers, radio and TV. Don't (just) get angry – get active!
- Show the video *Food for Life* at your school. It's aimed at teenagers and looks at how animals are farmed and the reasons for going veggie. Contact Viva! to hire or buy it.
- Persuade your friends and family to try going veggie during Animal Aid's 'Veggie Pledge Month'. Contact them for a free pack.
- Persuade your school restaurant to go meat-free during 'Schools'Veggie Week'. Contact Viva! for details.

- Adopt an animal – the Hillside Animal Sanctuary runs schemes to help raise money for all the rescued farmed animals they care for.

'To confine essentially wild animals in appalling conditions is a sad, sad commentary on the human race. A duck that never sees water – what an abomination. We have to stop this now.'
Twiggy Lawson, actress and former model

'Call ourselves a nation of animal lovers? What a joke! From birth to death, farm animals suffer. The only way forward is to stop eating them.'
Wendy Turner, presenter *Pet Rescue*

'Eating pork is obviously fatal – for the pigs. Need it be torture as well?'
Joanna Lumley, actress

'We can't go on cramming creatures into battery cages, broiler sheds, turkey sheds and so on. Where's the compassion? If you want to save animals, it's simple – support Viva! and go vegetarian!'
Sir Paul McCartney

Chapter 8

The Killing Fields

The Live Export and Slaughter of Farmed Animals

Jade Rossiter is 16 and recently joined a local animal rights group. She quickly found herself involved in something which was difficult to come to terms with.

'I was fed up with being all talk and no action so I decided to do something positive for animals. I joined a local group and started helping them with their campaigns. When I joined, the issue that seemed to be on everybody's mind was live exports. I have to be honest – to begin with I wasn't sure what it was all about. I knew that old, worn-out female sheep were being taken from the local hills where they'd spent all their lives, to market and sold. Most of those doing the buying were dealers and they took the sheep over to France and other European countries in big lorries where they sold them for big profits.

'That much I did understand. However, I found out that the reason the sheep were bought was so that people who follow the Muslim religion could kill them as part of a yearly festival. Apparently, they cut their throats while they are still fully conscious. Now that, I couldn't understand – why was it necessary, what was it all about and how on earth could anyone do it? Don't get me wrong, I don't want to criticise anyone's religion, but why would any religion involve killing sheep?

'A woman from a national animal-welfare group actually went over to France and watched this festival. It was in a big field just outside Paris (although apparently it took place in lots of other towns and villages as well, including a few in Britain). When she came back she gave a talk about it and I went along. I could hardly believe what I heard.

'Apparently this festival is centuries old and the sheep are a sacrifice to their God. She said that the atmosphere was like a holiday or carnival and thousands of families took part. The sheep that had been exported were held in big pens at the side of the field and people chose the one they wanted and paid for it.

'Some tied the sheep's legs together and carried it between them, some tied them and put them in wheelbarrows and others put a rope around their necks and dragged them along. But they all went to the same place – a pit covered with thick bars of metal. The sheep were dragged onto the metal, one man put his foot on the sheep's chin and held it to the ground while another cut its throat with a knife. Children stood around watching while this was done. The woman said that in some cases the people had knives that were too small or too blunt and it took minutes to kill the sheep. She showed some pictures and I wanted to be sick.

'After the sheep were dead, they were skinned, cut up into pieces and put in black bin liners which people took away with them, presumably to eat later. How such things can be done in the name of religion I will never understand.'

I might as well be totally upfront about this chapter – some people are not going to like it. I may be accused of all kinds of things, from religious intolerance to racism. Neither is true. I am tolerant of anyone's beliefs so long as they do not involve the abuse of animals or people. My own belief is very simple and it is that no person, no institution and no religion is above criticism.

There are two important issues in what Jade describes, the transport of living animals and their slaughter – in this instance ritual or religious slaughter.

Road to misery

In 1994, a most extraordinary thing happened in Britain. Animal welfare hit the news headlines every night of the week and it went on for months. What brought it about was the live export of calves and sheep by road, sea and air. TV screens were filled with the faces of frightened and confused calves and sheep, mooing and bleating pathetically as they peered through the tiny air slats in huge road transporters. The sheep were being sent abroad to be slaughtered while the calves were destined for Continental veal crates (see Chapter 7).

People from all over the UK took to the streets in places like Shoreham, Brightlingsea, Dover and Coventry and placed themselves in the road in order to stop the lorries. They were disgusted at a trade which treated animals as though they were nothing more than industrial spare parts. Officially they were considered to have no feelings and to be incapable of suffering.

The trade in calves from Britain came to an end when the rest of the world banned them for fear that they carried the mad-cow infection BSE. Sheep, unfortunately, have continued to be exported as part of a massive trade all over Europe.

In 1997, about 440,000 lambs and sheep were exported from the UK for slaughter and by 1998 it had increased to 700,000.

Exporters claim that their trade is governed by strict rules that ensure animal welfare but the facts are very different. Many of the animals exported from Britain are sent on horrendously long journeys and the welfare standards, both during the journey and when they're slaughtered, are often inhumane and illegal.

Compassion in World Farming (CIWF) have tracked many of these consignments of animals and have been shocked by what they discovered. In the summer of 1999, they followed thousands of sheep. After crossing the English Channel they were transported all the way across Europe – the whole length of France, over the Pyrenees mountains then down the entire length of Italy. At Bari, in southern Italy, they were transferred to a ferry and taken over to Patras in Greece where they were again loaded into lorries and transported to slaughterhouses.

In one case, the sheep were left in the lorry at Bari for 48 hours waiting for the ferry to arrive. The weather was blisteringly hot and the sheep had neither food nor, more importantly, water. CIWF investigators pleaded with the Italian authorities to unload and water the unfortunate animals. Eventually they did so but for many it was too late – 45 sheep and 115 lambs were dead.

Animals are rarely given food or water on journeys that can last 30, 40 or even 50 hours. They are crammed into lorries so tightly that any creature which loses its footing is likely to be trampled by others and die.

By the time the animals arrive they are stressed, thirsty, hungry and totally disorientated yet there is still no concern for their welfare. They are often unloaded brutally, being beaten, punched, kicked and often shocked with powerful electric goads. They are sometimes dragged by one leg into the slaughterhouses where they are often killed without first being stunned. The death rate on these journeys is high and the welfare conditions almost non-existent.

Perhaps the worst travellers of all are pigs who suffer terrible travel sickness, stress and dehydration after just eight hours. Even they are shown no mercy and can be transported for similar lengths of time.

In 1993, the European Commission itself admitted that its laws on the feeding and watering of animals in transit were 'systematically flouted'. Nothing has changed since then – the few rules on animal transport that exist are still ignored and the authorities simply turn a blind eye.

The Republic of Ireland is also heavily involved in the live-export trade and has developed new markets in North Africa, in particular Egypt and Libya. Unfortunately it's not easy to obtain information on the welfare of these animals, but with sea-journey times of up to 10 days, even longer in rough weather, it can be imagined.

Most of the animals that have to endure this journey are cattle. In a letter to CIWF, a boat skipper explains the process of travel sickness in cattle which are physically incapable of vomiting:

They are ruminants and digest their food by fermentation. When they are exposed to extreme motion, the fermentation increases and the gas production in their stomachs becomes excessive, resulting in the condition known as bloat. The whole abdomen becomes grossly extended, they suffer acute pain, falling down on the floor as they are flung around from side to side, grinding their teeth, moaning and groaning in agony, unable to breathe properly, until after hours or days of the most terrible suffering, their hearts eventually give out and, mercifully, they die.

A crying shame

The live export of animals portrays the human disregard for other life forms. One particular scene that has marked me, and many others, for life was the treatment of a young but fully grown bull, shown on national TV. He was slumped in the ship's hold in Croatia, his beautifully big and curly head looking around in obvious fear and pain. His pelvis had been broken. The handlers kicked and prodded but he was incapable of movement. One of them placed an electric goad on his testicles and delivered a 70,000 volt shock. The creature raised his head and bellowed a cry to rend the soul. It happened again and again for over half an hour. Each time he tried desperately to rise, scrabbling at the floor with his forelegs, but it was futile.

Eventually, still conscious, a shackle was attached to his foreleg and he was hauled up and out of the hold and dumped on the quayside. Pained and exhausted, he lay in a heap, unable even to raise his head. A debate followed between the ship's captain and the harbour authorities. It was decided it was more profitable to lose the beast at sea. He was hauled again into the air and dumped on the deck of the ship which then set sail. As soon as it was clear of the harbour, the bull was thrown into the sea. Whether he was alive or dead seems almost irrelevant after such treatment.

This routine brutality is an integral part of the international meat trade. Whenever and wherever a camera is turned on the transport and slaughter of animals it always comes up with images to disgust. Cruelty is commonplace and anyone who supports this trade by eating meat is directly involved in it.

What Jade witnessed was just one aspect of a European-wide trade in living animals. The method of slaughter she writes about is known as ritual or religious slaughter. In this case it was carried out by Muslims although Jews also slaughter animals while they are fully conscious. Ironically, this method of slaughter in both religions came about because of concern for animals. But before we talk about religious slaughter, it is important to know that the way billions of farmed animals are killed in Britain, Australia, the USA and most other industrialised countries of the world, isn't exactly a bed of roses.

The slaughterhouse

Most people don't want to work in a slaughterhouse, have never set foot in one and refuse to listen when you try to tell them about it. How much business would a restaurant do if, when someone ordered lamb chops, they were given a very sharp knife and a three-month-old lamb and told to cut its throat?

But the truth can only help people to make the right choices. So here it is!

Stunned

Slaughter, like any other business, is subject to all the usual business approaches – efficiency, incentives, cost control and so on. The animals that go through the slaughterhouse doors are units of production and the quicker they're killed, the higher the earnings and the greater the profits. Slaughter has become a production line just like a car factory.

Pigs, sheep and cattle arrive in lorries and are unloaded into a series of pens called a 'lairage'. Chickens are normally left in their crates to await slaughter.

Most animals are killed by having their throats cut and the rules say that they must first be stunned – made unconscious – to save them from feeling pain. Well, that's the theory but the drive for speed and efficiency results in the rules being bent. However, it is the methods of stunning themselves that make a nonsense of this supposedly humanitarian concern. Different methods are used for different animals. Some of them are:

- Electric tongs are used on pigs, most sheep and some calves.
- The captive bolt is used on cattle, most calves, some sheep and goats and, to a lesser extent, pigs and horses.
- An electrified water bath is used almost exclusively for poultry.
- Gas stunning is used on some pigs and poultry.
- Free bullet is used on most horses and deer.

Electric tongs

The animals are taken from the lairage to the stunning point, either individually or in groups, where they are penned and stunned one by one in front of each other. The low-voltage tongs consist of 'terminals', which look a bit like headphones, that are attached to insulated handles – imagine a large pair of garden shears with a round bit on the end of each blade. The slaughterman clamps the terminals to the animal's head, theoretically in front of its ears, and triggers an electric shock that is supposed to render it unconscious. A chain is then placed around a hind leg and the creature is hoisted into the air where its throat is cut ('sticking'), allowing it to bleed to death ('bleeding out').

The animal remains stunned for only about 20 seconds so if the slaughterman is too slow it can regain consciousness. Slaughtermen are usually on piece rates, being paid on the basis of how many animals they kill. To be truly effective the tongs need to be placed in exactly the right position on the animal's head and held there for at least seven seconds. For the sake of speed this often doesn't happen. Animals can and do regain consciousness within 20 seconds but often don't show it because one effect of the electric shock can be to induce paralysis for up to 30 seconds.

The Food Research Institute found that with sheep, the time between stunning and sticking was usually more than 30 seconds and in some cases more than a minute. What this means is that millions of animals are conscious when their throats are cut.

The European Union Veterinary Committee says: 'Under commercial conditions, a considerable proportion of animals are either inadequately stunned or require a second stun. This is mainly because of poor electrode placements, bad electrical contacts and long stun-to-stick intervals.' In some slaughterhouses the need for a second stun is ignored and in others it is done with a captive bolt pistol because by this time the animals have probably already been shackled and hoisted up.

Captive bolt pistol

There are two types of captive bolt pistol. The first is a little device like a pistol but when the trigger is pulled and the cartridge explodes, instead of firing a bullet it shoots out a metal bolt. The bolt can only travel 9 cm as it's still attached to the pistol. Cattle to be killed are driven one at a time into a roofless metal box, the pistol is placed against their forehead and the bolt fired into their brain.

With the second type, the end of the pistol is mushroom shaped. It is supposed to hit the cow's head with such force that it knocks her out, without entering the skull.

Used properly, both types of captive bolts will make the animal immediately lose consciousness but again, this often doesn't happen. A bad or hurried aim or a sudden movement from the animal and the bolt can miss, inflicting massive damage and terrible pain and requiring a second or even third attempt.

An investigation by Viva! in 2000 revealed that up to 10 per cent of stuns miss the mark in cattle abattoirs. This means at least 230,000 animals in Britain each year remain conscious when they are hauled up by a back leg to have their throat cut.

Electrified water bath

Poultry slaughter represents the ultimate in efficiency. They enter the 'packing stations' as living creatures and leave as wrapped, fresh or frozen table birds or in pies and other meat products. To feed this efficiency, a carefully planned production line is organised with lorries laden with crates full of birds arriving at set times throughout the day.

The chickens and turkeys have their legs placed in metal shackles and are hung upside down on a moving conveyor belt. Many of the chickens will already have broken bones. For turkeys, the shackling is particularly painful because of their weight, which can top 27 kg (about 60 lbs) in the case of overweight breeding birds – as much as an eight- or nine-year-old child. The strain on their usually diseased hip joints is enormous and painful.

The conveyor belt passes over an electrified bath and one by one their heads are dragged through it. Some birds miss the bath by raising their heads and these arrive at the human throat cutter fully conscious. The larger packing stations often use mechanical throat cutters and for smaller birds it can mean that the blade misses their throat and cuts their head while for larger birds it can mean a cut on the breast. If these failures aren't noticed it can mean that fully conscious birds are dipped into the scalding tank. This is a procedure which loosens the feathers and is another step in the relentless production line.

The Scientific Veterinary Committee of the European Union say they are concerned by this method of stunning because the wrong size shackles are often used; pre-stun shocks in turkeys are very high (80 per cent) because their wings hang lower than their heads and touch the water first; and currents may not be high enough to kill or cause unconsciousness. Heads of ducks and geese in particular may not be immersed in the waterbath at all because they are very good at 'swan-necking' – lifting their heads to avoid the water.

Gas stunning

In Britain in 1998, over four million pigs were stunned using a mixture of carbon dioxide and air. The welfare problems are severe. Pigs squeal, suffer extreme breathlessness and desperately try to escape for up to 30 seconds before they lose consciousness. The Scientific Veterinary Committee of the EU are concerned that pigs exposed to 90 per cent CO_2 take up to five minutes to die, but times vary and can be much longer.

Unfortunately the UK Government recommends that carbon-dioxide gassing is also used to stun ducks. However, a European Union report by vets contradicts their advice, stating that ducks suffer great distress if stunned with CO_2 and that this gas must be avoided! The Government shows inexcusable ignorance on this point as it is known that ducks are even less susceptible to CO_2 than other species.

One major UK broiler chicken 'processing plant' uses gas to stun poultry while they are still in their crates. The birds are not unloaded, shackled or knifed until they are dead. This should mean less stress for the animals so long as the gas mixture used is mainly argon, and no CO_2 is used. Even though it is known that using a CO_2 mix causes chickens to gasp, shake their heads and try to escape, it is still legal. Sadly for the poor birds, CO_2 is cheaper than argon.

Exacerbating the problem of inadequate stunning is the fact that many slaughterhouses do not train their staff. Viva! discovered that in the UK, one third of pig, sheep and cattle abattoirs give little or no formal training in animal welfare and half of the chicken abattoirs have no staff who have undergone formal training! This contemptuous attitude to animals simply beggars belief.

Vision of hell

It's one thing talking about slaughter but another witnessing it. I don't think anything could prepare you for the cloud of anger, disgust and despair you would feel. Viva! has managed to get inside several slaughterhouses. One was filmed over a few days and it defied the official position that if irregularities do take place they are infrequent. Irregularities were commonplace.

One incident, which made a huge impact on me, was seeing a young slaughterer pull a full-grown sow from a group of other jittery pigs by its ears and tail and then leap onto her back. Round and round ran the petrified creature while the youth rode her like a rodeo performer, yelling at the top of his voice. The nervousness of the other pigs increased, the pig being ridden panicked and the youth fell off her. He got up and kicked her several times in the stomach, then applied the tongs and she fell to the floor. He only kept the tongs in place for about three seconds and after she had been hauled up by her back leg, she could be seen struggling. He was still cursing her when he cut her throat.

Other footage showed a pig, covered in blood from its gaping throat, shake itself free from the shackles and fall to the floor where it ran around looking for a way out. The strange noises it made I took to be an attempt at squealing. As its blood drained away it gradually fell to the floor, was reshackled and hauled back up to continue through the production line.

In 2000, Viva! investigators visited an abattoir in the southeast of England. Sheep arrived and each was stunned with an electric shock for about two seconds. This was long enough to make the animals collapse, making it easy to chain their back leg but not long enough to render them unconscious when knifed. I saw one sheep violently kicking and lifting her head as she moved along the line, hanging upside down, blood spewing from her sliced throat.

Ritual slaughter

Both Jews and Muslims have special dispensation from the usual rules of slaughter in Britain, Australia, the USA and much of Europe. Animals killed to provide kosher or halal meat are sent to the knife fully conscious. This can be a slow and painful process for a stressed and terrified creature.

For Jewish 'shechita' slaughter, cattle are placed, one at a time, in a pen which holds them upright. The cow is pushed forwards so that its head sticks out one end; a plate moves up from the floor to support the underside of their body and its head is raised by a chin lift which extends the neck so that it can be cut more easily. When the throat has been cut, a side gate is raised and a hind leg is shackled. The chin lift and belly plate are released and the animal is pulled out of the pen by a hoist and moved to an overhead rail.

The animal is supposed to be killed instantly by a single cut across the neck. However, the reality is somewhat different, as the following description of secretly filmed Viva! footage of shechita killing shows:

The cow's neck is extended and the head lifted upwards by a chin lift in an upright pen; the animal's nostrils are flaring, eyes staring and it is salivating; the slaughterer cuts the cow's throat by slicing across it, backwards and forwards 13 times; the cow jerks away from the knife as far as it can and its facial reaction shows pain and great aversion; the cow does not collapse immediately... the filming ends before it does.

The problem with religious slaughter is that millions of animals suffer slow deaths. Scientists have documented how unstunned calves, which bleed poorly, can take a long time to die. Professor Donald Broom, specialist in farm-animal behaviour, University of Cambridge says: 'Animals are not stunned during the Jewish shechita or the Muslim halal ritual slaughter procedures. There is a period of consciousness after the throat is cut which may last from 30 seconds to *several minutes* during which the animal must be in great pain and distress. There is no logical reason why stunning should not be carried out before the throat is cut.'

For Muslim halal slaughter, sheep and goats are placed on their backs on a metal cradle or simply hoisted up by a back leg before having their throat slit. Poultry are held head downwards while their throats are cut.

Hardly surprisingly, many Muslims and Jews have turned against ritual slaughter and eat previously stunned meat or, much more effectively, have become vegetarian. The truth is that these killing methods originally came about through compassion. It is hard to believe but more than 2000 years ago, some people used to cut off part of a living animal for food – maybe the hump of a camel, the fat tail of a sheep or the leg of a goat – sterilise the cut with burning tar and let it heal. The poor animal would then survive to be killed another day and there were no rules covering how this should be done, either.

Religious leaders could see that this was unbearably cruel and so a series of religious laws were introduced. It was forbidden to slice bits off animals and when they were killed it had to be done quickly, with respect and in God's name. To ensure this happened, people were told that they must use extremely sharp knives, the animals mustn't be beaten or frightened and the whole process must be compassionate.

You could argue that killing animals can never be compassionate. Nevertheless, the whole motivation of religious or ritual slaughter was to save animals from suffering. Stunning the animals first was forbidden because at the time they didn't have any means of doing so other than beating them over the head, and that would have been cruel because it could have taken a long time.

The religious elders cared deeply about animals and wanted to protect them as much as possible but they could only do that with the knowledge they had available. Times have changed and stunning methods are available. This isn't acceptable to most of the followers of these religions because they insist that the rules laid down for killing can't ever be changed and so these centuries-old practices continue.

Some Jews and Muslims claim that meat from an animal killed by religious slaughter doesn't contain any blood and the process of stunning would leave some blood in the meat. This is important because their religions state that they shouldn't eat blood. In fact, if they truly didn't want to eat blood, they'd have to stop eating meat altogether because not all the blood drains away whether the animal is stunned or not. In fact, in non-religious slaughter the reason that animals are first stunned rather than being killed immediately is to allow the beating heart to continue longer, so that more blood is lost (this time for economic reasons, as bacteria in the blood causes the meat to deteriorate). However, it is now known that allowing the heart to continue beating makes no difference to the amount of blood lost. It is a tragedy that animal slaughter is based on so many misconceptions.

Any attempt to change the way animals are killed for both religions is fiercely resisted as if no change can ever be allowed. Of course, this is nonsense. In the Jewish religion, large animals such as cows used to be put in a metal crate called the Weinberg pen and turned upside down before being killed. Although this was known to be extremely cruel, religious leaders argued that it wasn't and that the practice could never be changed. It has been changed.

Similarly with Muslims, the festival Jade wrote about, 'Eid el Kebir', used to be a Jewish festival hundreds of years ago before it was adopted by Muslims. In those days, it was people who were sacrificed not animals but that, of course, no longer happens. So change is possible.

All the same, as I've already said, even when animals are stunned, things go wrong all the time. The only compassionate way forward is to go vegetarian and that's what many people of every faith are doing.

Cats and dogs suffer too

Cruelty to animals kept for meat is not limited to pigs and chickens, cows and sheep. In South Korea dog meat is considered a delicacy and only the wealthy can afford it. Men eat 'dog stew' in a questionable attempt to increase their sexual stamina and, although it is banned, it is consumed throughout the country. The meat is thought to improve in quality if the animal suffers a painful death. Three million dogs are electrocuted, blow-torched or strangled each year. At the places where dogs are strangled, metal collars are fitted to a wall a metre or more from the ground. The dog's neck is placed in the collar, its feet off the ground. The poor animal will try to climb the wall with its feet to keep the weight off its neck and this struggle for survival can go on for hours until it finally weakens and dies, hanging from the metal collar.

Another method is to beat it to death with an iron bar, again over a period of several hours. This suffering is supposed to tenderise the dog's meat and improve its flavour.

In China, cats are regularly eaten. The favoured method of killing is to plunge them alive into boiling fat and then strip their skin from them. Before you blame the Chinese for being particularly heartless, just remember that throughout Europe and the US, the accepted way of killing lobsters, crabs, prawns, shrimps and crayfish is to plunge them, alive, into boiling water. Animal cruelty has nothing to do with race but is all about culture. Some people, it seems, are just too insensitive to understand the basic concept of compassion. There are kind and compassionate people in all cultures who reject cruelty and work hard to end it.

In talking about these unbelievably cruel methods of killing animals I have tried to avoid emotion. It isn't easy and it doesn't show how I feel inside. It makes me feel physically sick and sometimes I despair for the human race. Fortunately, through my work with Viva!, I meet thousands of people who are making a stand, who are shouting 'enough is enough' and are determined to end the cruelty.

Success Stories

- Consistent campaigning in 1994 led to P&O Ferries, Stena Sealink and Brittany Ferries, the main cross-channel ferry operators, dropping the export of live animals for slaughter. The meat industry tried every possible outlet by air and sea, using the cover of dawn and dusk to move their fragile cargoes. But everywhere they went, at whatever time of day, people were there to greet them, to stand in their way, to lie in the road, to attack their consciences, to prevent their trade and to thrust the issue into the living room of every home in the country.

- More than 80 per cent of people in Britain are against religious slaughter.
- After years of campaigning, groups such as Viva! ended 'home' slaughter in 1999, stopping animals being ritually killed outside abattoirs.
- Norway and Sweden have banned all religious slaughter and Switzerland has banned it for mammals.
- In 1991 Korea passed its first animal protection law to outlaw dog meat and the International Fund for Animal Welfare (IFAW) is working with the Korean Animal Protection Society to close down the dog-meat dealers through public education.
- In 1998 the Animal Welfare Bill was made law in the Philippines, saving thousands of dogs from cruel deaths in meat markets, following a 16 year campaign by IFAW.

Action for Animals

- Go vegetarian or vegan and don't allow any animal to be transported or killed in your name. Contact Viva! for all the information you need to cut cruelty out of your diet (see Action for Animals in Chapter 7).
- Be loud and proud! Convince others to do the same

with masses of leaflets from Viva! and save even more lives. Going vegetarian or vegan is the best thing anyone can do to fight the insanity and cruelty of slaughter.

- Use ink to cause a stink! Write to your MP at the House of Commons, London SW1A 0AA and the government's Minister of Agriculture (responsible for farm-animal welfare) at the Ministry of Agriculture (MAFF), Nobel House, 17 Smith Square, London SW1P 3JR, asking for ritual slaughter and live exports to be banned.
- Also write to your local newspapers (listed under Newspapers in *Yellow Pages*) with a letter along the lines of:

Your name
Your address

Letters to the Editor
Newspaper's name and address

For publication

Dear Letters to the Editor

It is hard to believe but in Britain today millions of animals are slaughtered by having their throats cut while fully conscious. It happens quite legally, in the name of religion. The laws requiring all animals to be stunned before slaughter do not apply to those killed for the Jewish and Muslim faiths.

The victims are poultry, sheep, lambs, goats and cattle. The killing takes place in slaughterhouses serving this area and much of the meat is sold on the open market secretly, without any labelling. Anyone who eats meat is subsidising this barbaric practice.

Surely it is time to reform the law? Britain should join countries such as Norway and Sweden and ban ritual slaughter. Nothing – not even religion or tradition – can excuse cruelty.

Yours sincerely
Your name

- Support Compassion in World Farming's long running campaign to ban live exports. Join their vigil outside the government's Ministry of Agriculture in London or their demonstrations at Dover, where animals are loaded on to the ferries now privately owned by the farmers, to travel from the UK.
- Be in the know. Contact Viva! for their detailed reports *Sentenced to Death* on mainstream slaughter and *Going for the Kill* on religious slaughter.
- Kick up a fuss! Join a major initiative by Viva! to stop slaughter. Contact them for free stickers, postcards, leaflets, sample letters, posters, undercover footage of UK abattoirs and details of events and actions.
- Join IFAW's Korean dog campaign.

Chapter 9

Hook, Line and Sinker

Killing Fish for Fun and Food

Tony Moore loved sailing. He thought it was one of the most exciting things you could do. Well, at least he thought he did because he had never actually been. When a friend of his brother offered to take them, he jumped at the chance.

'The boat was in Brighton marina. It looked big enough tied up alongside all the other boats but it wasn't what I'd dreamed of. It was more the luxury, South of France, tanned film star kind of yacht I'd got in mind. Still, it was all that was on offer.

'The marina was huge and we didn't put the sails up at first; we just used the motor to get us to the sea. As soon as we passed the marina entrance, the boat started to go up and down as these big rolling swells of ocean came at us. Suddenly it looked like the littlest boat in the world. I checked my lifejacket and clung on.

'To be honest, it was incredibly boring sailing up and down and there wasn't much wind so we couldn't go very fast. When Pete suggested we drop the anchor and do a bit of fishing, I was quite relieved.

'We were about a mile from the shore and I could see the pier and the grand houses on the seafront and it all looked quite special. The wind had dropped completely, the sun was out, the sea was now smooth and I was really beginning to enjoy it.

'Pete and my brother got some rods out and fiddled around with hooks and things and finally dropped the bait over the side – horrible big, black wormy things. They didn't have floats or anything and I asked Pete how he'd know if he got a bite. He said to watch the end of the rod and it would jerk if a fish took the bait.

'I almost jumped up when the rod tip suddenly moved. It didn't just jerk, it rattled backwards and forwards like crazy but then suddenly stopped. "Pull it in," I shouted but Pete didn't move. He just said,"Not yet!"

'The rod tip went again and this time he jerked the rod up in the air and then started to reel in. "Got one," he said as though he was the big hero. I have to admit, I was quite impressed.

'I hadn't realised how clear the sea was and as I looked down through the water, I could see this silver shape flashing in the sunlight as it came up, getting closer and closer. Next thing, Pete swung it into the boat and it looked beautiful. I guess it was about 30 cm long. Then I noticed these little balloon things popping out of its head and suddenly realised they were its eyes. It was disgusting and I felt sorry for the poor thing.

'Pete took the hook out of its mouth and threw it back into the water. "Not worth keeping, it's a pout whiting – stink fish – not much good to eat," he said.

'I was relieved to see it hit the water and hoped it would swim back down to where it had just come from but it didn't. It kept trying to dive down but couldn't get more than a few centimetres below the surface.

'The current carried it away from the boat and when it was about 50 metres away, some seagulls came swooping in and starting pecking at it. The fish couldn't escape and it turned my stomach. The day wasn't nice any more – in fact it was appalling and all I wanted to do was get back on shore and try to forget about it.'

Human beings are fantastic at dreaming up excuses for abusing animals. They're pests, they're vermin, they enjoy the chase, they have to be controlled – you've probably heard them all before and you get the picture. But the greatest excuse of all is that fish don't feel pain.

The basis for this claim is that fish are 'cold blooded' but ask anyone who says this what it means and I bet they won't know. It has nothing to do with feeling or not feeling pain – it simply means that a fish's body isn't kept at a constant temperature like ours but changes according to the temperature of the water.

However, we are asked to believe that a complex animal with a central nervous system has no ability to feel the one thing essential to its survival – pain. The response that can tell it what will damage it and what won't is supposedly missing. They are saying, in effect, that the fish is the complete oddball of the animal kingdom – the only creature without a survival mechanism.

Without the ability to feel pain, the friendly little roach would swim straight into the jaws of a waiting pike, nestle among its row upon row of teeth, and smile while it was chewed to pieces. The myth that fish don't feel pain has been so successful that scientists have even picked up on it and have carried out experiments to see if it's true. Their conclusion is that fish are no different to other creatures – of course they feel pain.

Despite this, the 'painless' myth is still the excuse that

allows many anglers to justify their pastime. It is claimed that fishing is the most popular participation sport in Britain with some three million followers and that it is equally popular throughout the western world.

In fact, fish are incredibly sensitive creatures. They have very fine sensory hairs on their backs that can detect vibrations and electrical fields in the water. Often, they can see in the dark better than cats; their lips, snouts and throats contain millions of finely tuned taste buds; and they are extremely sensitive to odours. What anglers do is drive a crude, steel hook through these wonders of evolution – damaging, tearing, scarring and frequently introducing diseases through the open wounds.

No fun for fish

As with animal 'sports', there is a class system at work in fishing. Anglers divide their sport into three areas. There is coarse fishing for species such as pike, bream, rudd and tench which takes place on the majority of rivers, lakes and ponds; game fishing which is mostly for trout and salmon; and finally there is sea fishing for conger eel, shark, bass, plaice and cod. Since there are far fewer trout and salmon waters it can cost a lot to take part. As a result, game fishing tends to be for the wealthy, coarse fishing for the less wealthy and sea fishing is seen as the poor relation of both.

Coarse fishermen mostly put back the fish they catch while game fish and sea fish are usually killed and eaten. This is what, on the face of it, gives the coarse fishermen the moral high ground. 'We don't kill them,' they say, as if that makes everything OK.

Game fish are usually killed immediately but coarse

fish are often kept in small nets until the day's fishing is over when they are set free. They often die from suffocation because in the cramped conditions they are unable to get enough oxygen-rich water through their gills, or they damage themselves on the hard, knotted nylon net cord.

Rising to the bait

Fish are tempted to take a bait, hidden inside of which is a sharp hook. The bait might be bread, sweetcorn, luncheon meat, worms or maggots. In the case of game fishermen, the bait is usually artificial, made from feathers, tinsel and fur and designed to look like a fly or larva. Another method is 'spinning' which uses a piece of metal festooned with hooks. It is dragged through the water and is meant to look like a small fish in distress.

Some fish – those who are careful eaters such as carp – take the bait into their mouths slowly and when the fisherman 'strikes' (drives the hook home) the chances are it will tear into the fish's mouth. With smaller fish, it is not uncommon for the point of the hook to pierce the back of the eye and when the hook is removed, the eye is removed with it.

Other fish, particularly carnivorous ones such as perch, tend to bolt their food down quickly and, before the fisherman can strike, the bait is in their throat or stomach. That's where the hook ends up too, embedded deeply in soft tissue.

In order to deal with this, fishermen use a piece of metal called a 'disgorger'. It looks like a small knitting needle with a tiny fork on the end. It is thrust down the throat of the fully conscious fish in an attempt to dislodge the hook. It can take minutes, being pushed and pulled into the fish's organs with considerable force.

If the disgorger is successful and the hook is dislodged, pieces of flesh or intestine often come away attached to it. When it isn't successful, the fisherman pulls hard on the line until it breaks or tears free, leaving behind gaping wounds or ripping out some of the fish's intestines. Either way, a fish who has gorged a hook is likely to die an agonising death.

The cruellest use of bait is live bait – small fish impaled on hooks in the hope of catching larger, carnivorous fish such as pike. At least two hooks are used, one inserted in or near the head of the fish and one near the tail, and the aim is to keep the bait fish alive and swimming around attached to a float.

Bait fish may swim around like this for hours until they die from shock or are attacked by a predator. If, at the end of the day, nothing has been caught, the fish is simply torn off the hooks, tossed into the water and left to die. There is a lot of opposition to this method of fishing but it still goes on.

Vandals of the countryside

Fishermen like to present themselves as the saviours of the countryside but the truth is very different. Fishermen are one of the main causes of litter but it isn't just ordinary litter. Walk along any bank where they've been and you'll see it for yourself. Of course, there's the usual array of crisp packets, sandwich wrappers and drink cans but you'll also find old tins of sweetcorn and Spam, plastic bait containers and the plastic rings that hold 'four packs' together, all often fatal to birds.

The more serious damage is caused by the almost

invisible bits of fishing tackle that are often carelessly cast aside or left dangling from bushes and trees after they've become entangled. They are a terrible threat to birds.

The hooks may become embedded in their flesh, causing infections, swelling and even death. Birds may eat bait with a hook still inside which then becomes lodged in their intestines.

But it is the thin, nylon line which probably does the most damage. It doesn't rot so any that is discarded remains there for a very long time. Birds such as swans and ducks get the line entangled around their feet, wings or even beaks and can die slow and lingering deaths from starvation. Others lose limbs or wings as the thin line cuts through the flesh and bone or cuts off the blood supply.

For many years, the way of keeping bait on the river or lake bottom was to attach tiny lead weights called 'split shot' to the line. Often the weights were lost or just discarded into the water at the end of the day's fishing. This became the major cause of lead poisoning in swans and killed thousands of them in the 1960s and 1970s. Lead split shot also became a serious threat to the survival of the birds, who picked them up and swallowed them when they were sieving the mud with their beaks for food. These lead weights have now been banned but no thanks to fishermen who tried their hardest to blame motor-boat exhausts, shot-gun pellets and overhead power lines for the deaths of the swans.

Pop eye
Sea fishing involves many of these same assaults on fish and birds but there is one other cause of pain and death – and it's what Tony saw. Sea fish are often caught in very

deep water. At 100 ft or more down in the depths of the sea there is a lot more water pressure than on the surface. Because most fish live in just one type of environment, their bodies don't have the ability to adapt when they are forced into another.

When the sea fisherman hooks a fish on the seabed and hauls it up through the water, horrible changes take place to its body. Its swim bladder – a little capsule of air that ensures it stays upright when it swims – begins to expand. As the water pressure gets less and less, the closer to the surface the fish gets, the more the swim bladder expands.

The fluid surrounding the eyes and even the eyes themselves also enlarge until they balloon out of the poor creature's head. Other less obvious parts of its body also expand. The pain of this can only be imagined.

Even if the fish is tossed back into the sea, it will never be able to swim back down and is certain to die.

Even for fish taken from shallow water such as rivers and lakes, the pain of being hooked and the terrifying struggle for freedom must cause tremendous shock. To then be hauled out of the water into an alien environment, where its gills are incapable of supplying the oxygen it needs to breathe, must be even worse. It is a form of suffocation and must feel something like us being dragged under water and held there.

Every time a fish is caught and handled by the fishermen, the vital mucus which covers its scales is removed making the fish open to infection.

On coarse to cruelty

Thousands of coarse fishing competitions are held every year. At the end of the day, the catch of every fisherman is weighed. This can be a time-consuming process as the match officials adjust and readjust the scales to get the weight absolutely accurate. The fisherman might then want to have his or her picture taken with the prize catch. During this time the fish are gasping for oxygen and flipping around on the scale pans, possibly damaging themselves and certainly in great distress. It is only after all of this that the fish are killed or returned to the sea for their dubious fate.

A lot of people have an image of fishing as a quiet and peaceful pastime. Watch one of the many fishing matches that take place everywhere and you'll see a very different picture. It can be like a production line. Fishermen bombard the water with ground bait such as bread. It floats to the bottom and is supposed to attract fish around their hook which is baited with something much more attractive than bread. So much bait is thrown in that it can't all be eaten and often stays on the bottom, rotting and decaying and causing serious pollution.

I saw one match where anglers were trying to win not by catching the biggest fish but catching the heaviest weight of fish. They were catching bleak − a tiny fish a few inches long who tend to live in big shoals. They cast, they hooked a fish, swung it in, removed the hook, threw it in the keep net, re-baited and cast again − almost as quickly as you can read it. At the end of the day, the winner had over a thousand fish, every one of them damaged by the hook, handling, being crowded into a net and being traumatised.

One of the fishermen's latest demands is to have certain birds killed because, they claim, they eat 'their' fish. Top of the list are cormorants − beautiful black seabirds that can dive from hundreds of feet in the air, folding their wings by their sides as they flash through the water in pursuit of food.

One thing is certain, the fish's greatest disadvantage is the fact that it makes no sound. No matter how severe the torture and pain, it makes no noise. Believe me, if fish could scream, angling would be outlawed tomorrow.

The cruelty and devastation of 'sport' fishing, is over-shadowed by the global destruction caused by commercial fishing for food. This happens on every stretch of ocean or sea everywhere in the world.

All fishing methods are cruel but the old, traditional ones didn't threaten the survival of the oceans and all their inhabitants. In some parts of the world, you can still see these methods used. Spearing is probably the oldest method of all. Almost as old are bamboo traps that catch fish by the gills or bamboo tunnels that start off wide but become narrower and narrower. By the time the fish realises it, the tunnel is too narrow for it to turn around. Small circular nets, weighted with lead around the edges, thrown from canoes are also used and large semicircular nets are hauled in from the shore.

There are almost endless methods used for catching fish, including explosives and poisons. Both of these, of course, kill just about everything else in the area as well. But just as farming has become industrialised, so has fishing.

Industrialised fishing

Boats have become bigger, faster and more powerful which has meant that bigger nets can be used. Modern satellite technology and 'fish finders' – echo-location devices that actually show where the shoals of fish are – mean that fishermen don't have to waste their time fishing unless they know there are fish there. Modern fishing methods can wipe out a huge shoal of millions of fish in a matter of hours.

This is, of course, all incredibly sophisticated – the most efficient and biggest slaughter of the natural world in the planet's history. Across the world, about 100 million tons of fish are caught every year. As a result, the fish's fight for survival is getting more difficult every day.

Off Canada, 400,000 tons of cod used to be caught every year. Now they'd be lucky to fill a bucket with fish. Despite what everyone thought – leave them alone for a few years and they'll recover – they haven't. A similar, if not quite so bad, situation exists in the seas off Iceland.

We keep hearing the term 'overfishing' in the news. What this means is that fishermen take more fish from the sea than can be replaced by natural reproduction. Almost all of the world's major fishing areas are now overfished. The North Sea is cleared of a quarter of its fish every year – far more than can ever be replaced.

But still the killing goes on. And if you open almost any cookery or women's magazine, you'll find cookery writers still telling you to scoff as much fish as you can because it's good for you. They conveniently forget that some of the most poisonous chemicals known – PCBs and dioxins – are now in all fish, even those caught in the deepest and wildest oceans.

Sadly, it isn't just fish that are killed. Commercial fishing has also destroyed much of the oceans' environment in its chase after herring, cod, tuna, redfish and mackerel. Every few months a new report is issued by some big, concerned organisation like the United Nations, saying that the world's oceans can't sustain the onslaught and are dying. Even the organisation which represents fishermen — the International Convention for Exploration of the Seas — has said so.

Trawling tragedy

One of the main methods used is trawling. Trawlers slowly sail backwards and forwards across the oceans of the world, dragging nets behind them in a never-ending process. They scoop up huge quantities of fish and destroy the seabed and the creatures that live there.

The nets are huge tapering bags and the mouth of the bag can be 70 metres wide. It is kept open by huge, metal and timber boards, which weigh tons and crush and grind to destruction anything in their path.

Some fish escape the trawl by hiding behind small rocks on the seabed but the beam trawl has ended even their escape. A long metal beam is fixed under the mouth of the trawl and dangling from it are 'tickler' chains, which drag along the bottom forcing almost every creature from its hiding place into the mouth of the net.

The nets don't just catch edible fish, they also catch those that are too small or fish that no one wants. They bring to the surface just about every type of creature in the sea — brittlestars, sea urchins, crabs, sea anemones and even dolphins, seals and seabirds.

They are all shovelled back into the sea, dead or dying. Almost none of them survive.

Drifting danger

Drift nets are a different method of fishing and instead of catching fish on the seabed, they catch them near the surface. They're made from similar nylon line to that used by anglers and are just as invisible. They hang like huge net curtains from floats on the surface of the sea and can stretch for an incredible 50 km or even more.

The fish most commonly caught by this method is the poor old tuna – the most popular fish in the world. But the nets catch much more than tuna. Dolphins often feed on tuna so, naturally, they tend to follow them around. They also become victims of the drift nets, where they become entangled and drown because they can't reach the surface to breathe. Rays, sharks, seabirds and small whales all become entangled in these ghost nets.

Sometimes the nets become detached from their ships in rough weather and float away. But they still carry on killing large numbers of animals and birds. When heavy with the weight of dead bodies, they sink to the bottom of the ocean. Unfortunately, they don't stay there. Once the carcasses have rotted and the weight has reduced, the nets float back to the surface and begin their destruction again.

Up to one-and-a-half million dolphins, porpoises and small whales are destroyed by drift nets every year.

Purse seine – insane

Purse seine nets are also hung from floats on the surface but they stretch much further down into the depths of the ocean. The fishermen's electronic fish finders tell them where to float the nets and they form them into a complete circle hundreds of metres across. When the circle is complete, a wire at the bottom of the net is pulled tight and it closes, forming a kind of 'purse'. The fish have no escape and the net is hauled in.

Again, it's tuna who are often the target but many dolphins die as well.

★

Industrial fishing also has a terrible effect on other wildlife. Gulls, shags, razorbills, cormorants, kittiwakes and little auks feed mainly on sandeels, sprats and small herrings – the same fish caught by fishermen. There aren't enough fish for both and it's now common for seabirds to starve to death.

One thing fishermen never seem to do is blame themselves for the disappearing fish. It always has to be someone else's fault. The usual culprit is the seal. The problem of over-killing can only be solved by more killing, say the fishermen. As we've seen in Chapter 3, the result is that thousands of seals have been officially 'culled' – the polite word for bludgeoned to death – in Russia and Canada and there are calls for them to be killed in Britain.

Some people claim that fish farming is the answer. It isn't! In fact it's every bit as cruel and damaging as fishing. Nevertheless, fish farms have cropped up all over the world, including Britain and Europe.

Factory farmed fish

Fish farming is as intensive as factory farming animals on land and produces many of the same problems. Fish are crammed into netted cages or pens, usually in coastal waters, and their overcrowding leads to stress, disease and parasite infections, particularly of sea lice. The answer, the fish farmers say, is putting antibiotics in their pelleted feed, injecting a vaccine or bathing the fish in pesticides.

As if this wasn't enough, other disinfectants, fungicides, algicides and pesticides are also used in fish farms, as well as artificial colourings to make the flesh of salmon and trout a pretty pink, when really it is a dull grey (wild fish have naturally pink flesh from the crustaceans they eat).

The toxic build-up of stale food and this cocktail of chemicals destroys the environment and wildlife in the areas around the pens.

What happens when you cram fish together? Wildlife, such as otters, seals and seabirds, think it's their birthday and move in for supper – at which point the fish farmers kill them.

Another amazingly popular sea animal (for eating) is the prawn or shrimp. In some of the warmer parts of the world there is a huge industry in farming these little creatures. The areas chosen for the farms are usually places that have been seen as useless – mangrove-forest swamps. These are, in fact, anything but useless and are probably the most important areas of all the world's oceans.

About 90 per cent of all the fish in the sea start their lives in mangrove swamps and they are home to over 2000 species of sea creatures and plants. More than two thirds have been ruthlessly destroyed in the sub-tropical areas such as Indonesia, the Philippines, Malaysia, Thailand, Ecuador and Panama – the most important areas for mangrove swamps.

The crazy thing is that the farms cause so much pollution that after a few years they have to be moved and more mangroves are cut down. It's a large price to pay for a prawn cocktail!

Success Stories

- As always the campaigning of concerned people has brought about some important changes. Pisces, the anti-angling group, have persuaded many local authorities to ban fishing in their area or to stop the use of live bait and 'keep' nets.

- In an attempt to halt the declining numbers of fish, the European Union has agreed to cut the amounts that fishermen are allowed to catch. For example, from 2000 the Irish Sea cod catch has been reduced by 60 per cent; North Sea cod by 39 per cent; North Sea whiting and coley by 23 per cent; and haddock by 13 per cent.
- After a long campaign by the Whale and Dolphin Conservation Society and others, the European Union voted to ban drift nets throughout Europe. By the year 2001 the European drift net fleet has to be reduced to 25 per cent and then phased out – brilliant!

Action for Fish

- Don't eat fish. Contact Viva! for masses of help in changing to a cruelty-free diet.
- Use your gift of the gab – talk to anglers to destroy their concentration.
- Education is the key for the future. Contact Pisces for leaflets and posters, to join in National Anti-Angling Week, for a youth information pack and to arrange for one of their speakers to show their video *Angling: The Neglected Bloodsport* at your school.
- Write to the letters page of your local newspapers explaining how you feel about fishing. Watch out for any pro-angling replies and then respond yourself or ask Pisces to get on the job!
- Clean up! Litter threatens wildlife so why not do a clean up with some friends? Before you start, contact the local media – they may come and take a picture of

you working. Or you could join a conservation group – the British Trust for Conservation Volunteers organises trips to clear up ponds, canals and so on.

- Campaign against commercial fishing. Contact Viva! for their free pack against overfishing, including stickers and leaflets to educate fish eaters. Contact Animal Concern to join their 'No Fish Day' and work to stop salmon farmers from killing wildlife.
- Get clued up – contact Compassion in World Farming for their report *The Welfare of Farmed Fish*.

'I'm staggered at the rape of the oceans for fish.
Don't play a part in this senseless destruction –
don't eat fish.'
Pam Ferris, actress, *Where the Heart Is*,
Darling Buds of May

Chapter 10

Frankenstein Foods

The Genetic Engineering of Animals

Graeme Goldman, 15, describes himself as a cynic – someone who doesn't believe all that they're told. The problem is he can't always back up his doubts with hard facts, which can make life difficult at times.

'According to our science teachers, genetic engineering is the new penicillin – only more so. It's going to give us all a better future, increase food production and stop the environment from falling apart. And there's more! Animals and humans are going to be cured of diseases, there will be new medicines virtually on tap and there'll be all the organs you could ever want for transplants – the only problem is, they're going to be animal organs.

'If I'm honest, I don't really understand genetic engineering but the idea of using animals for spare parts just seems wrong to me. I can't quote you any science as to why it might be dangerous – I just feel it will be. But that's not really my objection, it's the idea that we can kill and slice up living creatures just because we can't be bothered to look after our own hearts and kidneys.

'When I try to talk about these things in class, I'm more or less laughed at. There's nothing wrong with genetic engineering – that's the message we keep getting from our science teachers and just about everyone in the class seems to agree. They just take it for granted that it's all going to happen.

'Even when I go home it's much the same story. When I to talk to my mum about it, she says that she has some worries about genetically modified foods and the like but she doesn't seem to know about the animals involved.

'My dad's a pharmacist and seems to think that he has to defend everything to do with genetic engineering. He seems to take it as a personal insult if you question science.

'Maybe my dad, my teachers and the scientists are right and my worries are all wrong. I know I don't have much knowledge but I still think there's plenty to worry about.'

Graeme might not know much about genetic engineering but his instincts are spot on. In fact there are plenty of scientists who feel exactly as he does.

All the evidence indicates that we have every reason to be concerned. Genetically modified organisms (GMOs) will be a disaster for the animals of the world. Millions are going to die in experiments and many more will be turned into freaks – grotesquely unnatural organ banks or food suppliers. There is nothing I can see that offers any hope for improvement in their lives but an awful lot that says their pain and suffering will be increased. There is some pretty strong evidence that it won't do humans much good either.

The two big questions are: Why are GMOs being introduced? And what exactly are they?

The first question is the easiest to answer. GMOs are being developed not because there's a big need for them but to make money. Pulling the strings are some of the biggest corporations in the world – in fact, some are so big that they have more money than some countries.

When you're that big and powerful, you have to keep growing all the time. If you don't, one of the other big companies will just swallow you up to help them get bigger. To keep growing and keep making big profits you have to come up with new ideas that give you an advantage over your competitors. If you can produce something that your competitors can't copy, so much the better.

All the big companies and governments have agreed between them that if whoever manages to create a new product based on GMOs, it belongs to them and them alone. This is 'gene patenting'. It's the perfect way to make money because you can then charge more or less what you like for the product.

Many of the biotechnology organisations involved in GMOs are pharmaceutical companies – those who develop and manufacture the world's medicines. They say they're spending billions on developing GMOs in order to cure diseases and save people's lives. However, they developed a cure for leprosy years ago but people in poorer countries still die from it because they can't afford to pay for the cure. Many of the 12 million children who die every year from diseases caused by starvation could be saved by a few pennies but their families are too poor to afford medicines. Some of the worst diseases in the world affect the very poorest people (such as parasite infections caused by contaminated drinking water). Perhaps it would be more effective if companies funded more programmes to alleviate these immediate problems.

It could seem that these companies only want to feed and cure the world's richer people – the ones who already have plenty of food and medicines, but also plenty of money.

Now to the second question. The principle behind GMOs is similar whether it's plants or animals that are being altered.

Plants and animals, including human animals, start from a single cell. At the heart of that cell is a nucleus. Packed inside it is a molecule of DNA (deoxyribonucleic acid) which contains genes. These hold the plan or 'blueprint' for how to build the plant or animal. It is genes that determine whether the cell becomes an oak tree, a jelly fish or a bear. There are genes for everything, from size to hair and eye colour.

As that single cell divides and creates new cells as part of the process of building the plant or animal, the DNA is duplicated each time. Every one of the millions of cells that eventually make you what you are contains DNA. 'Biotech' scientists are now altering this complex process.

They have already taken a tiny snippet of DNA from a fish called the flounder, and inserted it into a tomato. The snippet contains the gene responsible for preventing the fish from freezing solid in very cold water. The aim is to provide a kind of antifreeze for the tomato so it won't be damaged by frost.

They literally snip out the relevant gene from the DNA of a flounder cell and insert it into the DNA of a tomato cell. When the tomato cell starts to divide and grow, they hope that the new fish gene will also divide and grow as if it were a natural part of the tomato's DNA.

If that was all that happened, it might be possible for

the scientists to predict how the new DNA would act once it had grown into a tomato. But there is something else they have to do – another little but very important twist which makes genetic engineering very unpredictable.

The natural reaction of the tomato DNA would be to automatically reject the 'alien' fish gene so the scientists have to fool it into accepting it. They do this by covering it with a coating made up from a virus or bacterium that makes the gene invisible. They effectively smuggle it in.

Since there's a chance that the fish gene might just sit there and do nothing, they also have to include a 'promoter' to switch on the gene and start it producing its antifreeze. Since this process is difficult and often unsuccessful, the scientists also include a 'marker' gene that tells them whether they've been successful or not.

When it works, the world is changed. The simple tomato DNA, which has evolved over thousands or millions of years, is no longer just tomato DNA but one containing a fish gene, a virus or bacterium, a promoter gene and a marker gene. In other words it is a new creation which has never before existed in the entire history of the planet. It is something that could never have happened naturally. This is why people sometimes refer to these creations as Frankenstein's monsters.

Genetic engineering of animals is much the same as plants, only bloody and painful. Take cattle for example. A 'donor' cow is given a series of hormone injections to make her more fertile. She is then artificially inseminated with semen from a bull. Very soon after conception, the microscopic embryo is removed, injected with the new gene and then surgically implanted into another cow – the 'recipient'. The first cow may simply be killed.

After only a few days, the embryo is removed and checked to make sure that the changes have taken. If they have, it is surgically implanted into a third cow, the surrogate mother, who will carry the embryo for nearly nine months as it develops into a fully formed calf. Again, the second cow is likely to be killed.

Rather than risk infection through a normal birth, the calf is often delivered surgically – by caesarean section – and you can guess what happens to the surrogate mother afterwards. The scientists now have what they wanted, a 'transgenic' calf.

With farmed animals the success rate for the new DNA to switch on isn't very high, and it's estimated that as many as 40 animals may be used to produce one transgenic infant. Even then, there is no guarantee that it will have the right characteristics.

The three main reasons given for trying to produce transgenic farm animals are: for food; to provide organs for human transplants ('xenotransplantation'); and for medicines.

Munching monsters

Despite the fact that meat and dairy foods are linked to serious diseases in humans (heart disease, cancer, diet-related diabetes etc), the aim is to produce yet more animal products by boosting production. They are trying to produce animals with less fat and bigger, faster growing muscles. Even the 'successes' can be very cruel.

The Belgian Blue cow was engineered to make its offspring have bigger muscles around the rear end where the valuable steak meat is sited. It worked for the males but it produced females with a narrower birth canal, which resulted in great pain when trying to give birth to their babies. The calves have to be delivered by caesarian section. The same thing happens to the cows year after year, the scar tissue becoming more and more painful every time it is cut into.

A cruel bit of tinkering has been done to Swiss Brown cows. It was discovered that they have a genetic weakness which means they often develop a brain disease. When this disease flares up, oddly the cows produce more milk. When scientists located the gene that caused this disease they didn't use the knowledge to cure it – instead they made sure the cows got the disease just so they would give more milk!

US scientists incorporated human and cattle growth-hormone genes into lambs, hoping they would produce more meat more quickly. What actually happened was that the lambs developed crippled joints, a form of diabetes, and they died young. Other genetic engineers repeated the experiments and had similar results – all the lambs they produced died from diseases before they were one year old.

Believe it or not, scientists have tried to introduce a tobacco gene into sheep to act as an insect repellent. The most disturbing example of genetic engineering in animals that we know about (and there are plenty that we don't know about) also took place in the US. A human growth gene was introduced into the DNA of a pig in an attempt to produce more meat. The result was the Beltsville pig. This poor animal suffered so badly from arthritis that it couldn't even walk and had to crawl around on its knees. Most of the time it simply laid still, obviously distressed and in pain. It was also incapable of fighting off diseases. Despite this it produced young.

Cow growth hormone genes have also been put in pigs. The results were disastrous – gastric ulcers, liver and kidney damage, lameness, loss of co-ordination, poor vision and diabetes. Despite these failures, scientists in Britain, the US and Australia are continuing with similar experiments.

Another horrific experiment is the development of chickens to become almost featherless so that they can be kept in sheds in the heat of the desert.

One of the most incredible stories concerns milk and a genetically engineered growth hormone known as BST (bovine somatotrophin). It was made and sold in the US by the company that was so much in the news in the 1990s – Monsanto.

Cows were injected with BST every day in order to increase their milk output by up to 20 per cent without any extra feeding. Even during the experimental stages problems cropped up. A severe infection affects about one third of all dairy cows and causes an extremely painful swelling of their udders ('mastitis'). It happens because they are already producing more milk than their bodies can cope with. After being given BST to make them produce even more, it was found the infection got worse.

Monsanto attempted to sell BST in other countries, however scientists in Canada and the EU opposed this on animal welfare and health grounds. A panel of animal health experts appointed by the Canadian Veterinary Medicine Association found that cows injected with BST have an 18 per cent high rate of infertility, a 50 per cent increase in lameness, and are 25 per cent more likely to suffer from mastitis and die early (Consumer Policy Institute, New York, 15 January 1999 and Health Protection

Branch, Health Canada, Ottawa, 21 April 1999).

In March 1999, EU scientists announced that they had come to the same conclusion: 'BST administration causes very significantly poorer welfare...and often results in unnecessary pain, suffering and distress. The Scientific Community on Animal Health and Animal Welfare is of the opinion that BST should not be used in dairy cows.'

Further, a compound in cows' milk, called IGF-1, is known to play a part in causing some cancers. There was evidence, reported in the respected medical journal *The Lancet*, that cows treated with BST produced more of this chemical but despite this, Monsanto were given permission to sell BST to US farmers. Monsanto receive an estimated $300–500 million each year from sales of the hormone in the US, according to the Consumer Policy Institute in New York (Luke Anderson, *Genetic Engineering, Food, and our Environment*, Green Books, Totnes, 1999).

You'd think that BST would have been banned by the US government, but it wasn't. However, Canada, Europe and a number of other countries introduced their own bans. But why was BST even developed in the first place?

Both the EU and the US already produce far more milk than they can use. European governments actually pay some of their farmers not to produce milk (because they can't sell it all) and the US government buys up surplus milk and disposes of it to prevent the price from falling. The last thing any of these countries need is more milk!

Terror transplants

Xenotransplantation is the transplanting of organs such as hearts, liver and kidneys from animals into humans. When this happens, the natural reaction of the human body is to reject them. What scientists are doing is producing transgenic pigs which have been engineered with a human gene to make their organs seem more like human organs. It's hoped that these changes will fool the body into accepting the animals' organs.

This will pose a health risk for humans because pigs have viruses that are alien to us. By grafting bits of pig into human bodies, these viruses may infect us with potentially fatal diseases.

Life for the pigs is a chillingly cruel one. To produce animals for use in transplants, hygiene is obviously very important. Just at the point when they are about to give birth, the original mother pigs are killed and their womb containing the baby piglets is cut out and transferred into a sterile bubble. The piglets are reared in sterile, metal-floored cells – their home for life.

Meddling with medicines

The other promise of the genetic engineers is that by altering the genes of animals they will be able to produce medicine for humans almost 'on tap' in animals' milk. All kinds of experiments are currently underway, including a sheep which is supposed to produce a protein that prevents chest disease. It's now a waiting game to see what happens.

The very first genetic 'success' was in 1992 at Harvard University when scientists developed the 'oncomouse'. This little creature was bred to develop cancer after only six weeks of life, to save cancer research laboratories the trouble of creating cancer in their own, perfectly healthy mice (*New Scientist*, 26 June 1993).

Despite the pain and suffering endured by millions of these animals over many years, cancer rates keep on increasing. As we saw in Chapter 5, the biggest contributory factors to cancer are high-fat, high-meat and dairy diets; the second largest cause is smoking. The cure for most cancers is already in our hands!

Dolly folly

Once an animal has been engineered to produce whatever it is the scientists want, they can then create identical copies of it by 'cloning'. The nucleus from one of its cells is transplanted into a fertilised egg that has had its nucleus removed, replacing the missing nucleus. The egg is then cultured in the laboratory before being implanted into the womb of a surrogate mother. When it's time to give birth, again the mother is killed.

In 1997, the Roslin Institute in Edinburgh, Scotland announced that it had successfully cloned a sheep called Dolly. Scientists all over the world have been rushing to bring out their own clones and announcements of cloned animals are now regular events.

A French scientist cloned a cow that was already a clone herself. Just six weeks after the birth, there was a dramatic fall in the calf's red blood cells and a week later she was dead. When they examined her they found that her immune system had failed to develop properly.

One of the biggest dangers of cloning is that it works against the one thing vital to the survival of all animals – genetic diversity. If a small group of animals continually reproduces amongst themselves with no 'new blood', they rapidly develop diseases and die out. Cloning produces the smallest reproductive group ever known – one!

As I showed in Chapter 7, most food animals live in constant misery because they have been pushed to the limit. To push them even further with genetic engineering is a disaster for them.

The failures of this strange science read like chapters out of a horror novel but still the experiments go on. Added to all this are the possible effects of genetically modified crops. No matter what they say, no one really knows whether these inventions are safe or not. The majority of GM crops are fed to farmed animals so if anything is going to go wrong, it is the poor animals again who will be the first ones to suffer.

Some genetic scientists don't seem to concern themselves with the impact of their work on animals or the globe. We know from history that some scientists will do anything they can get away with and don't worry one jot about the morals. During World War II, some willingly carried out painful and brutal experiments on human prisoners. Therefore it is up to us, the ordinary people of the world, to decide what's right and what isn't.

Is it moral to inject hormones into a cow and cause her great discomfort for a product that no one wants? Is it moral to carry out agonisingly painful experiments on hundreds of pigs and then kill them in order to produce one that gains weight quickly, particularly when eating meat is causing great damage to the environment and human health? Is it moral to inflict pain on animals at all?

And should we be tampering with the genes of life that have taken millions of years to evolve?

We all have to make up our own minds. The world's environment is in crisis and its animals are disappearing at a terrifying rate. The people responsible are the same people who are now telling us that genetic engineering is safe. Do you believe them?

Success Stories

- An international Biosafety Protocol has been adopted worldwide in 2000 to control the trade of genetically modified organisms (GMOs). This has been a historic step towards protecting the environment and consumers from the dangers of genetic engineering.
- The demand for GM-free, organic food is increasing by 40 per cent a year in Britain. Parts of Austria are already 50 per cent organic and Denmark has launched a £200m initiative to treble its organic production.
- The UK chain stores, Marks & Spencer and Iceland have stopped buying products from animals fed on genetically modified crops.
- US farmers – who plant more genetically modified crops than any other country – are deserting GM. The amount of GM corn grown in 2000 dropped by one fifth from the previous year because of concerns over being able to sell GM foods.
- The biggest genetic engineering company in the world is called Monsanto. In 1999 farmers and environmentalists in the US and other countries joined together to bring legal action against Monsanto, claiming they sell genetically engineered seeds without properly testing how safe they are for people or the environment. The case continues.
- Despite a £1 million advertising campaign by Monsanto in Britain, the public opposition to genetic engineering has skyrocketed. The company is considering pulling out of Britain and Germany where supermarkets have turned their back on GMOs due to public pressure.

Action for Animals

- Go vegetarian or vegan. Contact Viva! for free info and be sure you're not eating genetically engineered animals or supporting horrific cruelty.
- Don't buy GM plant foods! Read food labels and avoid any products which are GM. Try to buy organic whenever you can – look out for the Soil Association's symbol on foods as it's the only scheme which guarantees products are truly organic and not intensively produced. (Organics Direct is a vegetarian company that delivers organic food to your door. Tel. 020 7729 2828; www.organicsdirect.com)
- Write to your MP at the House of Commons, London SW1A 0AA and the Secretary of State, Department of Health, Richmond House, 79 Whitehall, London SW1A 2NS to urge them to ban xenotransplantation. Point out that although there is a shortage of donor organs, animal transplants are not the answer. The situation could be improved if there was better promotion of the existing Donor Card scheme – currently only carried by 18 per cent of the British public – and a requirement by people to state their postition on organ donation when applying for a driving licence.
- Compassion in World Farming, the British Union for the Abolition of Vivisection and Uncaged are campaigning against using animal organs in people. Contact CIWF or BUAV for a copy of *Animal Organs in Humans* and Uncaged for *Xenoaction* ideas.
- Contact Greenpeace for a *True Food* campaign pack with free leaflets, stickers, petitions and posters.
- Support Compassion in World Farming's call for an

end to the genetic engineering of animals. Read their report, *Farm Animal Genetic Engineering*; hand out leaflets; display posters; arrange for a school speaker and ask your teacher to order their free *Genetic Engineering & Farm Animals* schools pack and video to educate the masses!

Chapter 11

In the Name of God

Animals and Religion

Anna Jarvis, 16, has been a vegetarian since she was eight years old. When her father had to go to Thailand to make a TV programme, she was over the moon when he asked her if she would like to go with him.

'I couldn't believe my luck. There was something magical to me about the whole idea of Thailand. And there was the added bonus that it is a Buddhist country and therefore vegetarian which would mean that for once I was in the majority.

'The film my dad was working on was about young Buddhist monks – novices – who start as young as 11 years old. It doesn't necessarily mean that they are going to be monks for the rest of their lives – it is often just a means of getting an education. Thailand is still quite a poor country in many parts and there's no guaranteed secondary schooling so if the monks accept you, you're guaranteed to get a very good education. It does mean, though, that you have to live like a monk.

'The boy we were following was 12 and I don't think he was very happy about being a monk. It meant he would see his mother only a couple of times a year and would never be allowed to touch her. I couldn't believe that to touch a woman, even his own mother, was somehow unclean and forbidden. But that was only my first shock.

'Monks are allowed to eat only the food that is given to them – it's called alms. They go out early in the morning – very early indeed – and we had to be at the monastery ready to go at 5 am. The young lad carried an alms bowl and a carrier bag slung over his shoulder.

'Off he went into the still-dark streets, the first glimpses of sunlight just appearing above the buildings. Some people set up little tables by the side of the road and on them were lots of little plastic bags containing food. At some of these tables there were queues of monks, each one holding out his bowl for bags of food. The people who give believe that donating food to the monks helps them reach heaven – 'nirvana'.

'When his bowl was full, the boy transferred his offerings to the carrier bag and then continued on his way. After a couple of hours his bag was nearly full and he headed back to the monastery. All the food was put together and shared out between those who had collected alms and those who hadn't, the young and the old. Then came my second shock.

'As they undid the little plastic bags and poured them out into bowls, I could see many contained fish or chicken curry. It didn't seem to worry any of them and they tucked in hungrily. Mind you, that isn't surprising since none of them had eaten since midday the day before. After midday they are not allowed to eat a thing until the following morning. They offered me some of the food but I didn't have a clue what was in it so I refused, even though I was absolutely starving.

'I'd always believed that Buddhists were vegetarians and here they were scoffing their way through pieces of fish and chicken and God knows what else, all donated by other Buddhists and they didn't seem to be in the slightest bit concerned. I really couldn't understand it and when I had the chance I tackled one of the monks about it. Of course, he didn't shake hands with me or anything like that because he wasn't allowed to touch me.

'He said that ordained (qualified) monks had to stick to hundreds of rules called 'precepts', but novices had only 12 precepts. Ordinary Buddhists, who weren't monks or nuns, didn't have to follow any rules at all. For them life was a process of learning and they would keep being reborn – reincarnated – until they had learnt how to lead a pure and holy life and part of that process was not taking any life.

'Now here comes catch 22. The monk claimed that because he was eating animals killed by someone else, he wasn't taking life. When I pointed out to him that by accepting dead animals in his alms bowl he was encouraging other people to take life, he said that one of the precepts that all monks had to live by was being totally humble and accepting whatever was given to them.

'I wasn't at all convinced by his answers. His English was good enough to understand me when I said I thought it was all a con. I could see he didn't like it when I said that it would be the easiest thing in the world to put the word out that the monks didn't want people to risk their place in the afterlife by killing animals for the monks. That would have stopped the whole hypocritical process dead in its tracks.

'I didn't realise it but my dad had been listening to all this and suddenly appeared. He thought it was time to whisk me away before I offended everyone. I got one last shot in and asked the monk if he thought it was right to encourage other monks to risk their salvation by accepting meat. I didn't hear his reply.

'For the next few days I went all over Bangkok, the capital of Thailand, and found it one of the most difficult places I've ever been to get vegetarian food. It was a real disappointment from that point of view. There were street sellers everywhere I went, cooking things in little pots by the side of the road. I think I saw bits of just about every living creature fried, boiled, steamed and grilled.'

I agree with Anna that one of the most difficult types of animal abuse to understand is that done in the name of religion. When the religion itself is opposed to all killing and cruelty, it makes it even more difficult to come to terms with. Wrapping animal abuse in a cloak of religion does not alter the fact that it is animal abuse (see Chapter 8). All religions have at their heart a belief in compassion and mercy. How that can be squared with the taking of innocent life is hard to understand.

Nearly all the great religions began at least 2000 or more years ago and to understand what they really thought about animals, it's best to look at the original teachings. In most cases, respect for animals was very much at the heart of them. Of course, once the original prophets died, there was no one with absolute authority to make up new laws or decide how their beliefs should be adapted to meet any change in circumstances. Because of this, the original teachings had to be 'interpreted' as time went by and those doing the interpreting were ordinary human beings – priests and other followers of the religion.

Stick a group of people with different views on a particular subject together in a room and ask them to reach agreement and you'll usually have a very long wait, particularly when it involves subjects like politics and religion where people hold very strong personal beliefs. It usually finishes up with an agreement to disagree, or a compromise that often fails to satisfy anyone.

This has happened to all religions over the centuries, so what is often presented as original teachings – rules set in stone that cannot be ignored or changed – are often nothing of the sort. They are frequently the beliefs of a small group of people, introduced into the religion many years ago but now treated as if they are the words of a god.

There's an old saying that in the Christian religion, you can prove anything you want by reading different parts of the Bible and there's a lot of truth in that. Of course accuracy isn't helped by the fact that most of the Bible wasn't written down until hundreds of years after Christ is supposed to have lived. But it's interesting that in the very first chapter of the first book of the Bible, it says: 'And God said, I give you all plants that bear seed every-where on earth, and every tree bearing fruit which yields seed: they shall be yours for food' (Genesis 1:29). It specifically doesn't say that He has provided every walk-ing, flying, crawling and swimming creature to be eaten.

The American group PETA (People for the Ethical Treatment of Animals) is so convinced that Christians are meant to be vegetarian that they have a web page called JesusVeg.com. Jesus was a vegetarian, they say. His message is one of love and compassion, kindness and mercy; he was not a butcher but a prince of peace – none of which squares with the pain we inflict on animals just so we can eat their flesh.

The first book of the Christian Bible states that the

Garden of Eden, God's perfect world, was vegetarian. Human frailty ensured it didn't last and it was followed by years of warfare, slavery, violence and flesh eating. But the prophets hadn't given up on reforming human weakness and the goal was to return to a peaceful and non-violent kingdom where 'even the lion will lie down with the lamb'. There are some Christians who say that the original writings, on which the Bible was based, were far more outspoken about animals and contained lots of passages actually outlawing eating them.

Although Christianity doesn't have any official laws stating how farmed animals should be killed, several unofficial Roman Catholic 'festivals' have grown up that ritually kill animals.

In one Spanish 'festival', a donkey is paraded into the village square and led to the church wall. The whole village then pile up against the donkey and press their whole body weight against it. They usually crush it to death. No doubt those responsible can offer some bizarre explanation but whatever it is, it's not acceptable.

In another Spanish village, a goat is led to the church and up the steps to the very top of the tower. It is then thrown from the tower. Young men and women on the ground below try to catch it in a blanket. Sometimes they fail and it is killed on the cobblestones. Sometimes they do catch it but its legs are broken and it has to be destroyed. Sometimes it survives.

Another example involves cloth soaked in oil and tied to the horns of a bull and set alight. Flames leap into the air and for half-an-hour or more the burning drives the bull into a frenzy as he tries desperately to escape. Eventually both his horns and his head burn, causing unimaginable pain to the poor creature. The actions of a terrified and confused animal are seen as a test of courage by macho men who run as close as they can to the thrashing horns and a source of amusement to the spectators.

The cruelty continues when, at another festival, a bull is surrounded by hundreds of people who blow sharp darts at it through a blow pipe. Eventually the pained and frightened animal is covered in thousands of stinging darts before he is finally hacked to death.

The religion that is perhaps closest to Christianity, and which had the same beginnings, is Judaism – the religion of the Jews. As with most religions, there are many splits and divisions based on how different priests ('rabbis') have interpreted the old teachings. It is proof that nothing is as clear cut as some would have you believe.

What is certain is that the Jewish religion includes great concern for animals. It actually forbids the deliberate causing of pain to them. Many Jews are vegetarian and believe that this is what God intended for humans.

Even IM Levinger, one of the main supporters of shechita – the Jewish method of killing animals (see Chapter 8) – agrees that many Jews are strongly opposed to the taking of animals' lives. There's a history of opposition and it's pretty strong stuff. In 1410, a religious leader called Albo said: 'Killing animals in order to consume their meat damages the human spirit.' In 1510, an elder called Abarbanel was just as outspoken: 'If the Torah allows the use of meat, it is only for people whose spirit is lost anyway.' (The Torah is a Jewish scripture and is the first five books of the Old Testament.)

Today, Rabbi Sidney Clayman says: 'The eating of meat in the Jewish dietary laws is not the ultimate goal but a concession to human weakness.' He states that vegetarianism is the ideal desired by God and all other standards are but stages towards it. The Union of Liberal and Progressive Jews states: 'Earliest man was expected to be vegetarian. . . there are many Jews [today] who regard the taking of animal life as morally obnoxious and consequently abstain from the consumption of any meat. Vegetarianism is the answer to their problem and indeed many outstanding Jewish personalities, past and present, have chosen this option.'

Eating blood and fat is a good example of how teachings can be interpreted in different ways. In the Torah it says: 'You shall eat neither blood nor fat.' This is the reason why Jews cut an animal's throat – so it loses its blood. However, it loses only about half of it. And fat isn't just the white stuff you can see, it is distributed throughout an animal's body, even in the red, meaty bits.

If you are to take that teaching literally, it obviously means you can't eat meat. This kind of unclear instruction and openness to interpretation runs through all religions. Surely you'd think that those who are religious would be wise enough to look at the spirit behind the teachings rather than trying to make sense out of each individual word? Unfortunately, that doesn't seem to be the way.

The Jewish Vegetarian Society maintains that if you go far enough back in history – way back to before Noah and the great flood – it was seen as a terrible thing to kill an animal. In fact it was considered just as evil as killing a human being and the person responsible would be put to death.

Their belief is that as the number of people in the world began to grow, God saw that humans were 'filled with violence' and decided to destroy the Earth. In the end God repented and accepted that humans were weak, but hoped that we would all eventually return to our original and compassionate ways. Presumably God's still waiting!

The world's most popular religion is Islam and those who follow it are called Muslims. In everyday life Muslims don't seem to show any greater concern for animals than other religions, yet if you read the original teachings animals are treated with great consideration.

The founder of Islam, the Holy Prophet Mohammed – who ate meat only five times in his life – laid out the rules in a holy book called the Quran (sometimes spelt Koran). Islamic teaching says that humans are the best of God's creations but puts a lot of responsibility on its followers to be kind, compassionate, merciful and charitable to all living beings. It is believed that animals possess a soul but that humans also have the capability of being spiritual – of understanding and worshipping God.

Humans have freedom of choice and their superiority over animals gives them the right, some Muslims say, to eat them. But there is a payback. If a person misuses this freedom of choice by being cruel to another human or an animal, they are immediately seen as the lowest of the low.

While most Muslims are not vegetarian, some are. The Muslim Vegan and Vegetarian Society says that the teachings of Islam implore Muslims to be compassionate to all animals. They say that the Prophet maintained that the three kingdoms – vegetable, animal and human – are all made of the same materials and are therefore cousins. Good Muslims should never do harm to any of them.

This kind of teaching is called a 'Hadith' – a collection of sayings of the Prophet – and there are many that refer to animals. They outlaw all vivisection, beating, branding, animal baiting, bloodsports and rough handling – even clipping a horse's tail is forbidden: 'It is its fly-flap,' said the Holy Prophet.

The Prophet Mohammed said that it was a great sin for humans to imprison those animals who are in their power. This, of course, would immediately outlaw factory farming. In fact, if the original teachings of Islam were followed everywhere, the world would be a much, much better place for all animals – an end to all vivisection, no more bear baiting, no more hunting, no battery cages or turkey sheds.

Sadly, that isn't the case, not even in Muslim countries. It seems extraordinary that some countries in which Islam is the predominant faith – such as Pakistan and Turkey – they still allow chained bears to be torn apart by dogs in the name of sport. It is in direct conflict with the teachings of the Muslim religion. And sadly this is the case with many religions. Their followers pick and choose which bits they will follow and which they won't. Usually, it seems, it's the instructions regarding animals which are the ones most readily ignored.

However, Buddhism theoretically turns its back on killing animals entirely and it isn't the only religion to do so. Vegetarianism is at the heart of the Hindu religion. Again, the higher up in the religion you are, the purer your diet is supposed to be.

An offshoot of Hinduism is Jainism. Jains claim they have gone back to the original Hindu teachings and refuse to purposely take any life at all – not even that of the tiniest insect. Some wear masks over their faces so they don't inhale flies as they walk along.

Another religion which stemmed from Hinduism is

Sikhism. While Sikhs are not required to be vegetarians, many of them are. There are very strict rules about how animals should be killed if they are to be eaten. They must be treated kindly and they must be decapitated (their heads chopped off) in one clean blow. I'm not sure that chopping an animal's head off can ever be kind. Sikhs are forbidden to eat meat killed by the Muslim method of slaughter, where animals' throats are cut while they are fully conscious (see Chapter 8). However, whenever I have been into a Sikh temple or community centre the food has always been vegetarian.

What seems true of all religions and all the great philosophers is that respect and compassion for animals is at their very heart. It is extraordinary that these beliefs were arrived at thousands of years ago when the world was a very different place – some would say a backward, primitive place.

If these teachings are 'backward' and 'primitive' then let's have some more of them. Perhaps these great philosophers understood even then how important it was to keep a natural balance in the world, something we now ignore at a terrible cost to the planet and all its inhabitants.

But let the Quran have the last word. It says that the person who destroys animals and plants and does so with clever excuses, even doing so in the name of Allah (God), then: 'Hell shall be their reckoning – verily it is a vile abode.'

Success Stories

- The 'festival' of throwing a goat from a church tower has been dropped from 2000 because of international pressure. A group called Fight Against Animal Cruelty in Europe (FAACE) run by Tony and Vicky Moore has been working for 10 years to end these spectacles of cruelty. They have forced regional Spanish governments to introduce new laws to prevent festival cruelty and have had some of the festivals banned and some abandoned. Sadly, Vicky died in 2000 from the after effects of a terrible goring from a bull she received when witnessing one of these spectacles. But the fight against cruelty by her husband Tony continues.

Action for Animals

- The Spanish Government is embarrassed by these festivals because they don't fit with the modern image they want to project. Increase their embarrassment by complaining about them. Whenever you hear of a cruel festival taking place, write a letter of complaint to the Spanish Embassy:
  The Ambassador of Spain
  Spanish Embassy
  39 Chesham Place
  London SW1 8QA
- Also write to your local newspapers (addresses in *Yellow Pages* under Newspapers), urging readers to also contact the embassy.
- And to your Member of European Parliament (get their name and address by calling 020 7227 4300). Ask them to pressurise the Spanish Government to ban all blood fiestas.
- Join FAACE's work to end Spanish blood fiestas.
- Ask your school to debate the attitude of different

religions to animals. Compare the original teachings with today's treatment of animals.

- Be smart and open-minded. Read some of the many books on religion and animals such as Viva!'s report on religious slaughter *Going for the Kill*; The Muslim Vegan and Vegetarian Society's *Islam and Vegetarianism*; the book *Vegetarianism: Living a Buddhist Life* (all available from Viva!) and The Fellowship of Life's booklet *Christian Vegetarianism*.

- Contact religious animal welfare societies such as the Jewish Vegetarian Society; the Catholic Study Circle for Animal Welfare; the Anglican Society for the Welfare of Animals; Quaker Concern for Animals; and Young Indian Vegetarians. (A full list is available from Viva!)

- Contact the Farm Animal Welfare Network (FAWN) for their leaflet against the battery farming of hens, which is signed by 25 bishops.

Chapter 12

Close to the Edge

Animals on the Brink of Extinction

Mass tourism and package holidays have had bad effects on some countries but they have also opened a lot of eyes to new and wonderful sights. Ranjit Patel, 16, is one who will never be the same again after an incredible holiday encounter.

'I got special leave from school to go on holiday one January. Mum, Dad, me and my sister were all off to the Gambia, in West Africa. It sounded really cool, really foreign. The thing I wanted to find out about was slavery because apparently this is where it all began. But there's no doubt about what I remember most – she was a five-year-old called Julia.

'We met by accident one day in a place called the Abuko nature reserve. We went there when there were no other tourists around because my mum knew the guy who ran the place. He showed us around on our own and took us to parts that other people never saw.

'We'd already seen loads of young chimps who'd been rescued from beach photographers – they were eventually going to be put back into the wild. But then, walking down a path in the trees, we came across Julia, walking hand in hand with her own special minder.

'The whole thing somehow looked just normal, a baby gorilla and a park keeper out for a morning walk! Julia came up to my waist and she sat down with us while her minder told us her story. It was like something out of James Bond.

'Her whole family group had been slaughtered by hunters but she was grabbed to be a pet. Somehow she had been sold from one person to another until she ended up in Belgium. The people who had her were looking to sell her to the highest bidder. Apparently she was worth an amazing £75,000.

'A wildlife group found out about her and the house where she was kept – a dark, dingy basement all on her own. I really don't like to think about how she'd got there or what she must have been feeling.

'(While the story went on, Julia decided I was her friend and lay across my knees on her back and kept fiddling with my ears and nose with her hard little fingers.)

'For some reason, the wildlife group couldn't just take her but had to get her into Holland first, a country next door to Belgium. They set up a complicated 'sting' whereby a couple of them pretended to be American buyers. They managed to persuade the people holding Julia that they were as corrupt as them and were genuinely going to pay out that kind of money. The kidnappers agreed to deliver Julia to a Dutch address.

'In fact, the rescuers were waiting on the other side of the border and as soon as the kidnappers came through the barrier, they pounced on them. Julia had been drugged and was hidden in the boot of the car.

'She is now part of a rehabilitation project and the hope is that one day they will introduce her to a wild gorilla family who will accept her. The problem is, Julia knows nothing about the wild and is having to be taught which fruits to pick and what shoots and leaves are good to eat.

'Julia had become fascinated by one of my hands and was holding and looking at it really closely. Her minder said not to let her put it in her mouth because although it was a friendly thing for her to do, she didn't know her own strength and might bite it badly. I felt her move my hand towards her mouth and I tried to stop her. I even used both hands but it wasn't any good. She was so strong my hand went straight into her mouth and she began to nibble it. Fortunately, she was really gentle and it didn't hurt at all.

'I looked at this beautiful not-so-little creature, sprawled out on me, happy as anything, and I felt ashamed to be human. I'll never understand how people can do such terrible things to such wonderful creatures.

'I know a lot of people feel the same way, like the wildlife group workers who risked their own safety to save Julia. Thank God for them.'

Half of all the creatures on this planet could shortly become extinct, simply because their homes are being destroyed by humans. And even the remainder aren't safe. One of the richest habitats for animals and plants is tropical rainforest but this is being destroyed at an incredible rate. Disappearing with the rainforest are all kinds of creatures, that are becoming extinct at the rate of 27,000 species a year – three an hour. And that's the most cautious estimate. The scale of the catastrophe is hard to comprehend but only by facing up to it can it be tackled.

Some people who make a living out of killing animals say that extinction is a natural process, and so it is, when left to nature. Species continually evolve and some will disappear and others be created. But what is happening now is *not* natural. The rate of extinction is 1000 times faster than intended.

There are between 10 million and 100 million species on Earth, only about one and a half million have been discovered. Most – tiny insects and single celled organisms, vital in recycling air, water and plant nutrients – will be gone before scientists even find out they were here.

The animals most at risk of extinction are big mammals – animals that produce milk for their young. Many are endangered but I'm going to look at just three: tigers, rhinos and gorillas. They can be seen as symbols of all the other species that may vanish shortly – unless we act now.

Tiger tiger, burning out

The tiger is the world's most charismatic predator. The breathtaking beauty and sheer strength of this magnificent cat holds a special fascination. Despite being known and loved by millions around the world, tigers are in desperate trouble. The total number has dropped by 95 per cent in the last century, with three types becoming extinct. The remaining five types are still falling in number and there are now only about 5000 left in the wild. If poaching continues at its current rate, there will be almost none left by 2010, the next Chinese Year of the Tiger.

Today, a mere 20 South China tigers remain, in the Russian Far East. About 415 Siberian tigers – the biggest species of cat in the world – cling to a perilous thread of survival, as does the Sumatran tiger in Indonesia, which numbers around 400. The Indo-Chinese tiger lives in Burma, Cambodia, Laos, Malaysia, Thailand and Vietnam, and numbers about 1180. The magnificent Indian, or Bengal, tiger is down to about 3000.

One major cause of the tiger's decline is the relentless destruction of its habitat. Massive areas of jungle are being laid to waste, leaving the big cats homeless and with no prey to eat. Its beauty is also its downfall, the tigers' pelts fetching very high prices. So-called 'sport' shooting – by people who find killing a rare species a macho challenge, particularly a strong, handsome animal like the tiger – is another reason for its decline. But the biggest threat of all is the illegal trade in its body parts, still used in 'traditional' Chinese medicine.

Some brave and dedicated conservationists risk their lives to try to stop the trade in fur and parts for medicine. They compile detailed dossiers on poaching gangs – finding out how they operate, which villagers and traders are involved and which politicians are illegally helping them in return for money. In India, they have found that cyanide is being used to poison small water sources in the relentlessly hot summer. Not only are tigers killed but all other wildlife that drink at the water hole. Other tigers are shot or snared.

One tragic consequence of the slaughter is the plight of the cubs left behind when their mother is killed. A tigress will usually give birth to two to four young and is a devoted mother. She suckles them for six months, never leaving them alone for long. After that time she encourages her cubs to join her on hunts. At first, young tigers are hopeless at killing and completely rely on their mother to teach them how to survive. At about one year old, the cubs will start to hunt alone but they stay with their mum until they are about two years old, or even four to five years old in the north.

Male tigers sometimes join the mother and her cubs (although not in Siberian tigers). The tigresses trust them completely, allowing them near the cubs. Contrary to their aggressive image, males will approach a mother and cubs when eating, attracted by the meat, but will wait patiently until all the others have eaten before tucking in.

Without their mother, cubs can't suckle or hunt. They are left to starve to death.

The Tiger Trust has followed the gruesome trade of body parts into China and found that the bone is used for arthritis, 'devil possession', and eruptions under the toenail; the eyeballs are used for fevers in children; tiger genitalia are prescribed for male impotence; the tiger's nose is sometimes hung above the marital bed in parts of China to induce the birth of boys; and the blood is believed to strengthen willpower. The claims lack any scientific proof.

It's hard to believe this 'medicine' trade could be so damaging until you look at the staggering scale of it. In three years, China illegally exports *27 million items* of tiger products. South Korea, Taiwan and Japan also illegally trade in a huge volume of tiger parts. In South East Asia poachers can earn up to $6000 for a tiger skeleton – about three times the average yearly salary.

Some people try to excuse the persecution of the tiger by saying that the Chinese have been using tiger parts since time immemorial. But how can tradition justify cruelty and the wiping out of a species? In fact, using tiger parts on such a wide scale is a fairly recent thing.

The tiger was so despised that in the mid 1950s the Chinese authorities classed it as 'vermin' and set out to annihilate it. In the 1960s, some people struck on the idea of selling the stockpile of tiger carcases to make themselves a fortune. They reworked old 'medicines' previously known only to the very rich – the mandarins and emperors – and marketed them successfully to the masses.

When the pile of tiger parts ran out at the end of the 1980s, poachers began killing tigers in the forests of India and smuggling them into China. This international trade has been banned for about 25 years and China supposedly outlawed the selling of tiger parts in 1993. But it will take strong action by governments rather than empty words to stop this despicable trade.

Horn of darkness
Rhinoceros means 'a horn on its nose' – and it is its horn that has caused this animal's decimation.

There are five types of this plant-eating, intelligent giant remaining but each is threatened with extinction. The black rhino and white rhino live in Africa; the Javan, Indian and Sumatran rhinos in Asia.

The poaching of rhinos in Africa has been ruthless and constant. The numbers of black rhinos have plummeted from 60,000 to only 2500 in the last 20 years. The southern white rhino numbers 6750. The northern white rhino lives only in Congo's Garamba National Park where the situation is grim. Only 24 animals survive, making it practically impossible for this awesome creature, which has lived on Earth for 60 million years, to recover its numbers.

The Javan rhino is also one of the rarest mammals on Earth, with just 75 animals remaining. The number of Sumatran rhinos has nosedived to 500. There is a glimmer of hope, however, for the Indian rhino, whose population has increased from 12 in 1908 to 2000 today. This success is due to the protection provided by reserves, which were set up mainly to conserve the tiger.

Rhinos are called 'nature's tank' – a pretty good description when you see them charging at 50 km per hour through dense thornbush, scattering a herd of elephants! Even stalking lions will break off a hunt to detour around rhinos. Not surprisingly, adult rhinos have no predators – except humans.

All rhinos need water, not only for drinking but to keep cool. By wallowing in pools or mud they keep their skin clean and wash away insects. Black rhinos live on the grassy plains of Africa, and Javan and Sumatran rhinos roam beautiful Asian forests. They all eat twigs and leaves, using their horn to pull down branches, and they enjoy fruits that have fallen from trees. In contrast, Indian and white rhinos eat grass. (Confusingly, white rhinos are the same colour as black rhinos – grey – but have a different shaped mouth.)

Baby rhinos suckle from their mothers until they are about a year old. Like the tigress, a rhino mum is very protective, using her horn to threaten any potential attackers. When young white rhinos are ready to leave their mother, they often find an old female (called an aunt) to take care of them. An aunt will look after three or four young.

Sumatran rhinos try to keep as far away from people as possible by going into the deepest part of the forest. Very sensible! They are amazingly agile, climbing the steepest parts of the mountains where people can't follow.

Like the tiger, the rhino has been massacred by

humans: for 'sport'; by the relentless destruction of its natural habitat; and for its horn.

As human populations have increased, wildlife has correspondingly decreased. When there is competition for space, humans always win, often at the expense of all else. The Javan rhino used to live in lush forests all over Sumatra and Thailand but when the forests were destroyed, the starving animals raided farmers' crops. The governments responded by annihilating the animals. The 75 survivors all live in just one national park on the island of Java.

Although reserves have been created for all rhinos and it is against the law to kill them or to trade in horn, poachers still threaten their survival by secretly slaughtering them for their horn. Wires connected to powerlines are dangled across rhino paths, electrocuting the animals who walk into them. It is a cruel and agonising death. Others are shot by well-armed men who then chop off their horn, leaving the bodies to rot.

The driving force for the destruction is again China, which pays high prices for the horn for use in 'traditional' medicine. A kilogram of powdered African rhino horn fetches about £2500, while a kilogram of horn from Asian rhinos is worth a staggering £32,000. Some Chinese believe that rhino horn cures sore throats, fevers, bad backs, rheumatism, arthritis and other illnesses. Pieces of rhino skin, toenails, blood and dung are also highly prized.

North Yemen has also wreaked havoc on the rhino. In the 1970s, the country imported 40 per cent of the world's rhino horn for 'djambias', dagger handles. Many of the finest – elegantly studded with gold and silver – are worth more than $10,000. Boys are given daggers at 12 years old when they traditionally become men. Because the country is wealthy from selling oil, many families can afford rhino horn daggers. The poor person's equivalent comes from cattle horns. Today this trade still continues illegally, but it is dwarfed by China's voracious appetite for horn.

Gorillas to be missed...

The bushmeat trade is the most serious threat to the survival of gorillas. It also threatens chimpanzees, bonobos (pygmy chimps) and forest elephants.

In the past, the market for bushmeat – the meat of wild animals – was limited because it was difficult to access the dense forests of West and Central Africa. However, humans have trashed so much of these rich wildlife environments for cattle grazing, logging and building, that it's become much easier to target their inhabitants and the demand for the meat is growing.

The gorilla shares 97.7 per cent of our genes. Like it, and the chimpanzee, we too are classed as a great ape (nothing so great about us, you might say!). Eating a gorilla or chimp is tantamount to cannibalism. Yet humans are eating our fellow apes to extinction. What does that say about us as a species?

The gorilla is the largest of the great apes. There are three races: the mountain, the western lowland and the eastern lowland gorillas, which all live in equatorial Africa. Around 600 mountain gorillas live in the Lake Kivu area, in the rainforests and bamboo forests of the mountainous landscape; 10,500 eastern lowland gorillas live only in the rainforests of the eastern Congo; and

111,000 western lowland gorillas inhabit the rainforests from Cameroon to the Congo river.

Gorillas are vegan and have a very similar digestive system to humans. They enjoy tucking into leaves and the hearts of stalks, roots, fruit and shoots. They live mainly on the ground in groups of 6 to 20, with 1 or 2 male leaders plus females, infants and young adult males.

The group usually eats between about 7 am and 9 am and then rests for a couple of hours. Too restless for sleep, the young play a game similar to 'catch', or they might defend a tree stump against the assault of others – much like 'king of the castle' and other games played by human children. The group sleep, eat, groom and 'talk' all after-noon and then, at dusk, they build a nest by bending the stems of grasses and bushes and settle down for the night. Their life expectancy in the wild is 30 years.

Rarely has a creature been so badly misunderstood as the gorilla. All the stories about them being fierce killers – spouted by hunters to excuse their trade – are nonsense. These truly are gentle giants. They are non-aggressive and shy animals, unless frightened or when defending themselves.

The adult males have a saddle of silvery grey hairs on the lower part of their back, which gives them their name 'silverbacks'. These strong males are double the weight of females and make threatening displays at intruders to protect their group. They beat their chests, roaring and rush at the intruder several times but this is usually followed by a discreet withdrawal.

A group of gorillas is never seen fighting with other groups. If they cross the same territory, the leading males may just stare at each other but even this is rare. They are happy to coexist. Unlike some other primates, male gorillas within a group rarely squabble between themselves, not even over mating. The group leader may even tolerate another male flirting with a female only a few metres away from him. They may even have sex – apparently a rather noisy affair!

What makes gorillas so vulnerable to extinction is that a female only gives birth to one baby once every four years. Her pregnancy lasts eight and a half months and so a quick recovery in numbers for a small population is impossible. The mother gorilla will handle her new born baby with love and care, holding her or him closely to her chest. If a baby dies, mothers can show desperate grief. One mother was seen holding her dead baby for four days before being able to let go.

Gorillas are peace-loving, sociable animals and obviously feel the same range of emotions as humans. Their annihilation is repulsive and cruel. When hunted, the male leader is killed first. The females are then encircled and clubbed to death. It is pitiful to see how, to fend off the blows, they only hold their arms above their heads. They are sold for meat, and their babies sold as 'pets'.

There is a ragged army of 2000 bushmeat hunters in West and Central Africa. They butcher over 3000 gorillas a year. They use clubs, guns, snares and spears. Gorilla meat can be found in food markets throughout the region. Their body parts are also used in various 'witch-doctor' medicines. For example, the World Society for the Protection of Animals (WSPA) found that dried gorilla hands are ground into a powder and sprinkled into babies' baths to make them strong.

As with tigers and rhinos, the killing and trading in

gorillas is illegal. However, while a gorilla carcass sells for £20 and a gorilla hand for £1, the killing will continue. Although these sound like small sums to us, to African poachers it is a small fortune. The orphaned babies sell for £40 which encourages hunters to shoot mothers. For every baby gorilla sold, 50 will have died en route. And of course the babies grow quickly ending up in chains in someone's backyard or dumped.

It is not only Africans who are to blame. Multinational companies encourage cattle grazing where the forests once grew. European and Asian logging companies, which profit from selling the precious rainforest trees, build roads deep into the forests which the hunters then use for access to kill the wildlife. These same big companies often don't supply their workforce with food, encouraging them to buy bushmeat. Sadly, there is hardly anywhere left for the gorillas to hide.

The fate of all animals depends on how we humans manage the environment. Are we going to continue to rob nature or is there any hope that we will begin to appreciate and value the preciousness of life? Our species has the power to destroy the Earth but we seem unable to recognise that all things are connected. We are dependent on plants, animals, water and soil for our existence. The fight for the survival of tigers, rhinos and gorillas represents the fight for the Earth. It is a battle we *have* to win.

Success Stories

- In Thailand, two sanctuaries have been established which care for orphaned tiger cubs. It's impossible to train the cubs to hunt in the way their mothers would have done and so they can never be returned to the wild. However, Tiger Mountains One and Two are the biggest enclosures in the world and contain bamboo groves, shady copses, mountainous rocks and pools with waterfalls, which the tigers love to play in.

- In Russia, a World Wildlife Fund (WWF) anti-poaching brigade protects about 50 Siberian tigers. The brigade goes out for four to five days at a time, carrying out raids and confiscating any tiger products, which are burned after being used as evidence in court. If they find any illegal guns, these are also destroyed.

- One man caught selling a tiger skin, was sent to jail for two years. The team has blocked trade from one of the main routes from Russia to China, reducing the number of tigers killed from 70 a year in the early 1990s to 15 a year today.

- The WWF also supports seven reserves in India, having recently spent £500,000 on strengthening anti-poaching work and providing vehicles and other equipment. They also manage the reserves, lobby the Indian government and prosecute poachers and traders. They will even prosecute the government if it fails to meet its legal requirement to protect the tiger. There is also an education programme for children and eco-projects and schemes to involve local villages in the fight to save the tiger. It runs similar schemes for rhinos and gorillas.

- At the end of the last century, the southern white rhino was thought to be extinct. However, a few were discovered in South Africa and after vigilant protection they have increased to 6750 animals, the healthiest population of rhinos alive today.

- The production of a gun cartridge – the powerful chevrotine used illegally to kill gorillas – was stopped by the WSPA. This has reduced the impact of hunters who use guns but, of course, traditional hunters have never used guns.
- Some major wildlife groups formed the Ape Alliance in 1998 to work together to protect gorillas and chimpanzees. They are pressurising European logging companies to help stop the hunting of gorillas in the forests that they are destroying.

Action for Animals

- When abroad, don't buy trinkets made from animals, particularly from endangered species. If you see any, call the police in the area that you see the trinkets; if the trinkets are for sale in a European country also contact your MEP (Member of the European Parliament – get their name and address by calling 020 7227 4300). And contact a wildlife organisation such as the WWF, Born Free, Care for the Wild or WSPA. Remember to write down the address of where they were for sale. You could also do this if you see any in your home country.
- Adopt a tiger at Tiger Mountain or a rhino at a reserve. You'll receive a certificate, photo, tiger or rhino T-shirt, leaflets and fact sheets. Your money will be used to care for 'your' cub or rhino and to fund anti-poaching teams. Contact Care for the Wild.
- Ask your school to support the WWF's tiger, rhino and/or gorilla projects. The WWF have colourful packs for teachers as well as leaflets, posters, ideas for action, videos and more.

- Ask our government and India's government to do more to stamp out the illegal trade in tiger and rhino parts. Write to your MP (find out her or his name by calling the House of Commons Info Line on 020 7219 4272) at the House of Commons, London SW1A 0AA and MEP (details above), and to:
The High Commissioner
Office of the High Commission for India
Aldwych
London WC2 4NA
- Help apes Escape! Join the WSPA's 'Escape' campaign to support sanctuaries for orphaned gorillas and chimps, and to work with governments to use the law to end hunting and confiscate gorilla 'pets'.
- Don't buy wood or any timber products unless they have a stamp of approval from the Forest Stewardship Council. The FSC is the only independent scheme which ensures wood has come from forests where gorillas and other wildlife have not been affected.

Conclusion

Why Does it Matter?

'What are we without the beasts? If the beasts were gone, we would die from a great loneliness of the spirit. For whatever happens to the beasts soon happens to all people. All things are connected. Whatever befalls the earth befalls the sons and daughters of the earth. We did not weave the web of life, we are merely a strand in it. Whatever we do to the web we do to ourselves.'

These words are more than 150 years old and were said by Chief Seattle, a native American Indian. Today we can put people on the moon and fly across the globe in jet aircraft but most of us fail completely to understand his simple truth.

Does caring about animals and wanting to protect and defend them matter? It is, I believe, the most important thing we can do. Without care, concern and compassion for all living creatures, humans stand very little chance of surviving. Perhaps the only question left if we don't change our ways is how much damage we cause to the planet before we finally disappear. I want to show here just how much all living things are inter-related.

There are simple and obvious reasons why all animals have a role to play. In some states of North America, such as North and South Dakota and Colorado, coyotes (a kind of wild dog) were considered pests because they occasionally attacked young farmed animals. The same kind of hysteria that is used to demonise foxes in Britain erupted and these beautiful creatures were portrayed as evil vermin. Anyone could kill them, anyhow, anywhere – and they did, until they were virtually wiped out.

The same people then started to complain about prairie-dogs. These little creatures aren't dogs at all but are more like squirrels. They burrow beneath the ground and were a favourite food of coyotes. With the coyotes gone, prairie dog numbers blossomed and farmland was badly damaged by their burrowing. It caused far more damage than the coyotes ever did.

The answer you would think would be to bring back the coyotes. But no, poisoning and shooting were used again – not very successfully as it turned out. If it had been successful and the prairie dogs eliminated, nature's balance would have been disrupted even more and another, unforeseen problem would almost certainly have developed. It is this simple fact – that all things are related – that most people don't seem to understand.

In China 40 years ago, its leader, Mao Zedong, decided that birds were eating far too much grain. The whole country embarked on a campaign to kill all grain-eating birds, and they were fairly successful. The next year's harvest was almost destroyed by insects because there were no birds to eat them. The policy was reversed.

In the UK, farmers were rewarded with cash for being 'efficient'. That meant producing more and more food from bigger and bigger fields. Trees, hedgerows, ponds and woods were all destroyed to make way for these huge, soulless prairies. The outcome was a disaster – not such an obvious one but a disaster nevertheless. To produce more food the land was swamped with herbicides and pesticides – poisons to kill weeds, insects and fungi. The financial cost was extremely high.

Then, of course, someone discovered that in small fields bordered by hedges, far less pesticide was needed because predatory insects that lived in the hedgerows were able to spread out into the fields and colonise them, feeding on those insects that damage crops.

Now, the same farmers who were rewarded for causing the problem in the first place are being paid for putting beetle banks in their big fields. These strips of raised land are left to nature so that beetles and other predators can make their homes in them, spreading out into the fields to feed on the pests. They are, in effect, mini-hedgerows but without the hedges or trees, which would also have provided homes for birds and other creatures.

Since World War II, we have swamped the land with industrial and agricultural chemicals. At one time, nearly all birds of prey were facing extinction because some of these chemicals had made them infertile. Even as I am writing this chapter, a UK daily newspaper has carried a shocking story. One of its reporters, who is young, has a healthy diet and exercises regularly, has sent some of her cells to be tested in a laboratory. They discovered that in one single fat cell, there are more than 1000 different polluting chemicals.

They found traces of highly poisonous pesticides and

233

toxic industrial chemicals, some that affect fertility and others linked to birth defects. It's highly likely that this poisonous cocktail will be passed on to any children she might have, possibly concentrating and becoming even more damaging.

We have no idea what the long-term effects of this poisoning might be but one thing we do know is that it is entirely unnatural for the human body. It is possible that we will all eventually pay the price for it in terms of sickness and disease. The source of this incredible assault is the attitude that regards nature and the natural world as irrelevant or something to be controlled entirely for our benefit.

I believe that as a species we have set ourselves up almost as gods of the globe. It is only *our* needs and wants that are important. Everything else is there either for our use, our profit or our entertainment and nothing has a right to life. We are the ones who decide what will live and die and how.

We slaughter owls, hawks, crows and magpies so that grouse or pheasants can be bred in large numbers. We then kill them by shooting them out of the sky with shotguns and call it sport. We call foxes vermin and destroy them in horrible ways. When the rabbits on which they feed then increase in number, we also call them vermin and kill them too.

We gas badgers because they might be diseased with TB. We trap and kill rooks because we don't like their habits; chase hares with dogs for entertainment; do anything we like to rats and mice; and shoot pigeons in their tens of thousands. Across the globe we chase whales and harpoon them for 'cultural' reasons; we destroy dolphins and seals because they dare to eat fish. There is hardly a species we won't annihilate if their interests clash with ours.

We decide which animals we will eat and deny them everything. By selective breeding, genetic manipulation and interfering with their diet, we are producing farmed animals that can't even live without our support. At the same time, we are destroying the wild gene pool from which they came.

By regularly using powerful drugs and antibiotics as if they were nothing more than sweeties, we are producing superbugs – bacteria that cause poisoning for which there is no cure. By playing with the lives of other animals, we are risking our own.

It seems we are incapable of understanding that every living creature has its part to play in keeping this wonderful world of ours healthy. None of the animals we slaughter, even those we call vermin, offer any threat to the survival of the planet. The only animal which does that is us – human beings.

For centuries we have run the world on this basis – that it is only us who matter. The result is extremely frightening. Over the past few years, several reports have been issued on the state of the world. They have come from serious and reputable sources such as the World Health Organisation, Oxfam, the World Watch Institute and the United Nations. The warnings in these reports are blunt – the natural world is dying at a terrifying pace and there isn't much time left.

The planet has existed for something like 5 billion years but human beings have been here for little more than a twinkling of light by comparison – about two million years. If you reduced time to just one year, the earth having been created on January 1st, human beings didn't appear until a few seconds to midnight on December 31st.

Although we began to change the face of the planet just a few thousand years ago, the speed of that change has been accelerating all the time. It really began to pick up pace no more than 200 years ago but for the last 50 years it has been like a fully loaded lorry tearing down a steep hill without brakes. This is the period during which contempt for animals and the natural world has been at its worst and most damage has been done. It affects land, sea and air, and everything we do to the planet affects its animals and eventually us as well.

The air we breathe is polluted by industry and above our heads there are far more dangerous changes taking place, but we can't see them. In the stratosphere, the layer of gas called ozone filters the sun's direct rays, preventing the most damaging light – ultraviolet light – from reaching the earth's surface.

Ultraviolet light has the ability to cause deadly skin cancer and cataracts, which can seriously damage eyesight. It isn't only human eyesight which is at risk but that of all mammals. It also attacks the immune system, making it more difficult for us – and animals – to fight off disease.

It reduces the germination of seeds, putting plant growth at risk and it can kill very young fish. There is real fear that it may destroy the tiny specks of vegetable growth (phytoplankton) that form the basis of the ocean's entire food chain. If that dies, the oceans die, and if the oceans die we die.

Holes have appeared in the ozone layer, allowing up to 40 per cent more ultraviolet light to reach the earth and the damage is beginning to show. Even though there has been some control over the chemicals that reduce ozone (CFCs), it looks as if they will continue to be released into the atmosphere for at least a further 70 years.

The Earth's cooling system is also under attack by other gases – mainly carbon dioxide and methane. They have effectively thrown a blanket around the world and prevent heat from leaving its surface. They have a similar effect to a greenhouse, holding heat in. The result of this greenhouse effect is global warming. It is leading to a change in weather patterns almost everywhere, melting the polar ice caps and warming and expanding the oceans.

The result will be a rise in sea levels which will flood large areas of land, making as many as one billion people homeless. They will have nowhere to go so will have no choice but to move on to other people's land, causing great upheaval and putting even greater pressure on the natural world.

All the world's oceans are being overfished and there is a knock-on effect on other creatures. Animals such as seals and dolphins that have lived side by side for perhaps millions of years are beginning to attack and eat each other because of lack of food. Seabirds are starving to death and all the animals that depend upon the sea are under tremendous pressure for survival.

On land, existing deserts such as the Sahara are spreading at an ever-increasing rate – and one third of the world's land surface is rapidly turning to desert because of overgrazing by farmed animals. In most countries, the fertility of land is dropping because of intensive agriculture.

Rainforest and other natural habitats, and the animals that live in them, are being destroyed ever faster. There is no longer enough fresh water for the world's people and reserves are disappearing fast as it is squandered on watering livestock. The University of California reckons that the amount of irrigation water needed to produce one pound of vegetables is 25 gallons whereas for a pound of beef it is 5000 gallons. We are using the resources of the Earth in a completely inefficient way with our dependence on meat. The great rivers of the planet are drying up, partly because of the demands of the growing numbers of thirsty farmed animals.

It is a very depressing story indeed. No wonder 75 per cent of all the world's animals are either declining or facing extinction. As we've seen some great and magnificent creatures such as tigers, rhinos and gorillas are almost without hope. If we can't save animals so big and obvious as these, what hope is there for the thousands of other creatures, some of which we have never even seen?

Even now, if you talk about animal rights or express concern for animals, there are plenty of people who will tell you your priorities are all wrong. They will tell you that humans must come first. Even now, after all that's gone wrong and is still going wrong, they can't see that to care about animals is to care about humans. We both share the same environment. If something is wrong for one, it is wrong for both.

The philosophy of greed and selfishness, which turned animals into nothing more than commodities, has been a terrible failure. The same people who pretend that humans must come first are often the same ones who are quite prepared to exploit humans as well as animals. Just look across the world and you will see that care and concern for humans is almost as rare as it is for animals.

While 12 million children die every year from starvation, there are people with so much money they don't know what to do with it. The gap between those who have and those who have not grows wider all the time. It is the people responsible for the destruction of the globe who tell us there is no alternative. They are also the ones who benefit from things as they are, in the short term at any rate.

We have listened to them for too long and even now, when the world and all its wonderful inhabitants are dying at a terrifying rate, they still insist they are right. What's even worse, they claim that the same policies which got us into this mess – free markets and consumerism – are the same policies that will cure it. It's like a quack doctor recommending bleeding as a cure for a severe haemorrhage.

We can save the world but we have to change our thinking. We need to cherish animals and the places where they live. It is much more exciting and fulfilling to quietly watch a vixen as she plays with her cubs as they scamper and tumble in the spring sunshine than to chase her across the countryside on horseback and laugh while she is torn to pieces and her cubs thrown to the hounds.

To discover the paw prints of a tigress and her young in the dried mud of an Indian river is more enriching than any tiger-skin trinket; far more important than swallowing her ground up bones and pretending it's medicine. Trying to understand the huge range of a whale's speech, far more complex than our own, is infinitely more satisfying than blasting it to death with an explosive harpoon for its oil.

You should carry your concern and love for animals with pride because you are telling the world that there is a better and more compassionate way of running things. You are the hope for the future and if we who care about animals are not successful, the destruction will continue until it is complete. It is a fight against ignorance, greed and selfishness and there is nothing on your side except truth, compassion and determination. But then, these are the most important and powerful weapons of all. It is a fight for life – a fight we have to win!

Directory of
Animal Groups

The world's largest database of animal protection societies, with over 10,000 listings and links to more than 3000 websites is at www.worldanimal.net

United Kingdom

For a full list of animal groups in the UK, contact Viva! for a copy of *The Animal Contacts Directory*, £4.95 (plus £1 p&p) or see website www.veggies.org.uk

Advocates for Animals
10 Queensferry Street
Edinburgh EH2 4PG
Tel: 0131 225 6039
advocates.animals@virgin.net
www. advocatesforanimals.co.uk
Campaigns against all animal abuse including the abolition of vivisection.

Animal Aid
The Old Chapel
Bradford Street
Tonbridge TN9 1AW
Tel: 01732 364546
info@animalaid.org.uk
www.animalaid.org.uk
Concerned with all aspects of animal abuse, it has a great youth section and local groups across the UK.

Animal Cruelty Investigation
Group
PO Box 8
Halesworth IP19 0JL
Tel: 01986 782280
Fax: 01986 782551
mike@acigawis.freeserve.co.uk
www.acigawis.freeserve.co.uk
Investigates and exposes all cruelty to animals.

Animal Defenders
261 Goldhawk Road
London W12 9PE
Tel: 020 8846 9777
navs@cygnet.co.uk
www.cygnet.co.uk/navs
Investigates animal suffering and
campaigns against all animal
abuse. Part of the National Anti-
Vivisection Society.

Arcnews
PO Box 339
Wolverhampton WV10 7BZ
Tel: 01902 711935
james@arcnews.co.uk
www.arcnews.co.uk
News from local animal rights
groups throughout the UK.

The Blue Cross
Home Close Farm
Shilton Road
Burford
Oxford OX18 4PF
Tel: 01993 825502
www.bluecross.org.uk
Cares for and rehomes abandoned animals with 11 adoption
centres for all companion
animals; also has two equine
centres and five hospitals to treat
animals of people who can't
afford private vet treatment.

Born Free Foundation
3 Grove House
Foundry Lane
Horsham RH13 5PL
Tel: 01403 240170
Fax: 01403 327838
info@bornfree.org.uk
www.bornfree.org.uk
International wildlife charity.
Includes the Zoo Check project
which exposes the suffering of
captive animals in zoos, circuses,
dolphinaria and gives them practical help; Elefriends which
battles to save the elephants; the
Big Cat Project which rescues
wild cats from captivity and
conserves animals in the wild.

British Trust for Conservation
Volunteers
36 St Mary's Street
Wallingford OX10 0EU
Tel: 01491 839766
Fax: 01491 839646
information@btcv.org.uk
www.btcv.org.uk
Runs conservation holidays all
over Britain.

British Union for the Abolition
of Vivisection (BUAV)
16a Crane Grove
London N7 8LB
Tel: 020 7700 4888
info@buav.org
www.buav.org
Campaigns to abolish experiments on animals.

Captive Animals' Protection
Society
PO Box 43
Dudley DY3 2YP
Tel/Fax: 01384 456682
caps-uk@dircon.co.uk
www.caps-uk.dircon.co.uk
Exposes the suffering of animals
in circuses and lobbies councils
to ban animal acts.

Care for the Wild
1 Ashfold
Horsham Road
Rusper
Horsham RH12 4QX
Tel: 01293 871596
Fax: 01293 871022
info@careforthewild.org.uk
www.careforthewild.org.uk
Aims to protect wildlife from
cruelty and exploitation and to
alleviate suffering, for example by
providing direct aid to wildlife
reserves.

Cats Protection League
17 Kings Road
Horsham RH13 5PN
Tel: 01403 221900
Helpline: 01403 221927
cpl@cats.org.uk
www.cats.org.uk
A cat-rescue organisation with
14 shelters and 240 voluntary
branches that rescue and rehome
75,000 cats each year. Encourages

caring ownership and neutering
and has a junior mag.

Coalition to Abolish the Fur
Trade
PO Box 38
Manchester M60 1NX
Tel: 07939 264864
caft@caft.demon.co.uk
www.arcnews.co.uk
A grassroots organisation helping
to co-ordinate local actions
against the fur trade. Carries out
investigations, campaigns and
political work.

Compassion in World Farming
(CIWF)
5a Charles Street
Petersfield GU32 3EH
Tel: 01730 264208
info@ciwf.co.uk
www.ciwf.co.uk
Actively campaigns against
farm-animal cruelty. Produces
Farmwatch newsletter for 10 to
16 year olds and has local groups
throughout Britain.

Dr Hadwen Trust for Humane
Research
84A Tilehouse Street
Hitchin SG5 2DY
Tel: 01462 436819
staff@drhadwentrust.org.uk
www.drhadwentrust.org.uk
Anti-vivisection group

fundraising to provide grants for non-animal research.

Elefriends (see Born Free Foundation)

Environmental Investigation Agency
2nd floor, 69–85 Old Street
London EC1V 9HX
Tel: 020 7490 7040
info@eia-international.org
www.eia-international.org
Research, investigation, campaigns on pilot whaling, the ivory trade, pets and endangered species.

Farm Animal Welfare Network
PO Box 40
Holmfirth
Huddersfield HD7 1QY
Tel: 01484 688650
Research, information, campaigns and lobbying on welfare of farmed animals.

Fight Against Animal Cruelty in Europe (FAACE)
29 Shakespeare Street
Southport PR8 5AB
Tel: 01704 535922
action@faace.co.uk
www.faace.co.uk
Campaigns against Spanish blood fiestas and bullfighting.

The Fox Project
The Old Chapel
Bradford Street
Tonbridge TN9 1AW
Tel: 01732 3655340
robmel@innotts.co.uk
www.innotts.co.uk
A charity which works in SE England to speak up for the fox and to rescue injured animals. It also operates a humane deterrent to stop foxes going in the gardens of those people who would hurt them.

Friends of the Earth
26–28 Underwood Street
London N1 7JQ
Tel: 020 7490 1555
www.foe.co.uk
Campaigns on environmental issues; has many local groups.

Great Ape Project
PO Box 2602
Reading RG2 7YQ
Tel: 0410 124987
gap@envirolink.org
www.envirolink.org/gap/home.html
Works for increased protection for great apes by lobbying for basic moral and legal protection that only human beings currently enjoy.

Greenpeace
Canonbury Villas
London N1 2PN
Tel: 020 7865 8100
gp-info@greenpeace.org
www.greenpeace.org.uk
Campaigns to protect the environment at home and abroad.

Hillside Animal Sanctuary
Hall Lane
Frettenham
Norwich NR12 7LT
Tel: 01603 736200/891227
hillside@mailgate.ftech.net
www.hillside.org.uk
Rescue centre for farm and other animals; also works to end intensive farming.

Humane Research Trust
29 Bramhall Lane South
Bramhall SK7 2DN
Tel: 0161 439 8041
Members@Humane.freeserve.co.uk
www.btinternet.com/~shawweb/hrt/
Promotes and funds medical research without the use of vivisection.

Hunt Saboteurs
PO Box 2786
Brighton BN2 2AX
Tel/Fax: 01273 622827
info@huntsabs.org.uk

www.huntsabs.org.uk
Campaigns and direct action against all blood sports.

Hunt Saboteurs Youth Group
Animals Freedom
PO Box 127
Kidderminster DY10 3UZ
Tel: 01562 700086

International Fund for Animal Welfare (IFAW)
87–90 Albert Embankment
London SE1 7UD
Tel: 020 7587 6700
www.ifaw.org
Worldwide campaigns against the abuse of animals and their environment.

Jewish Vegetarian Society
855 Finchley Road
London NW11 8LX
Tel: 020 8455 0692
jvs@bmjjhr.easynet.co.uk
http://easyweb.easynet.co.uk/~bmjjhr/jvs.htm
Info service on going vegetarian and related issues.

League Against Cruel Sports (LACS)
83–87 Union Street
London SE1 1SG
Tel: 020 7403 6155
mail@league.uk.com
www.league.uk.com

Campaigns to ban bloodsports, often by lobbying politicians. Also owns wildlife sanctuaries on which all hunting is banned.

Monkeyworld Ltd
Nanoose
Longthornes
Wareham BH20 6HH
Tel: 0800 456600/01929 462537
Fax: 01929 405414
apes@ape-rescue.org
www.monkeyworld.org
Assists foreign governments to stop the smuggling of primates from the wild. Primates are rehabilitated into natural living groups at the Centre.

National Anti-Hunt Campaign
PO Box 66
Stevenage SG1 2TR
Tel: 01442 240246
nahc@nahc.freeserve.co.uk
Campaigns and publicity stunts to expose the cruelty of hunting.

National Anti-Vivisection
Society (see Animal Defenders)

People's Dispensary for Sick
Animals (PDSA)
Whitechapel Way
Priorslee
Telford TF2 9PQ
Tel: 01952 290999
pr@pdsa.org.uk

www.pdsa.org.uk
Britain's largest veterinary charity, giving free treatment to animals of disadvantaged owners. Has 120 charity shops selling donated items all over the UK. Their youth group, Pet Protectors, produces a great mag, *Animal Antics*.

People for the Ethical Treatment
of Animals (PETA)
PO Box 3169
London SW18 4WJ
Tel: 020 8870 3966
info@peta.demon.co.uk
www.petaonline.org.uk
Vigorous campaigns throughout Europe on vivisection and all animal abuse in partnership with USA group.

Pisces
BM Fish
London WC1N 3XX
Tel: 01792 464176
pisces@pisces.demon.co.uk
www.pisces.demon.co.uk
Campaigns against angling.

Protect Our Wild Animals
(POWA)
23 Tormount Road
Plumstead
London SE18 1QD
Tel: 020 8316 7852
Formed in 1998 for the purpose

of reminding New Labour of
their pre-election pledge to ban
hunting with dogs.

Respect for Animals
PO Box 6500
Nottingham NG4 3GB
Tel: 0115 952 5440
respect.for.animals@dial.
pipex.com
www.respectforanimals.org
Campaigns against the fur
trade and against cruel food
production.

Royal Society for the Prevention
of Cruelty to Animals (RSPCA)
Causeway
Horsham RH12 1HG
Tel: 01403 264181
24-hour number for suspected
cruelty cases: 0870 55 55 999
webmail@rspca.org.uk
www.rspca.org.uk
Britain's most wealthy animal-
welfare charity. Has more than
300 inspectors who investigate
cases of cruelty and may prosecute. Produces fantastic junior
magazine. However, Freedom
Food scheme for farmed animals
allows factory farming.

Save the Rhino
Winchester Wharf
Clink Street
London SE1 9DG

Tel: 020 7357 7474
save@rhinos.demon.co.uk
www.savetherhino.com
Conservation group, eg funding
anti-poaching teams.

Soil Association
Bristol House
40–56 Victoria Street
Bristol BS1 6BY
Tel: 0117 929 0661
Campaigns for organic animal
and plant food production and
against genetic engineering, use
of chemicals, antibiotics etc.
Runs an organic certification
scheme.

Sustain
94 White Lion Street
London N1 9PF
Tel: 020 7837 1228
sustain@sustainweb.org
www.sustainweb.org
An alliance of food, farming,
animal-welfare, environmental
and public-health groups, aiming
to promote sustainable farming.
Publishes reports, eg on the
impact of animal farming on
animals and the environment.

Uncaged
14 Ridgeway Road
Sheffield S12 2SS
Tel: 0114 253 0020
uncaged.anti-

viv@dial.pipex.com
www.uncaged.co.uk
Campaigns against animal
experiments, including xenotransplantation.

Vegan Society
7 Battle Road
St Leonards on Sea
TN37 7AA
Tel: 01424 427393
info@vegansociety.com
www.vegansociety.com
Lots of information on vegan
nutrition, health, recipes and
products.

Viva!
12 Queen Square
Brighton BN1 3FD
Tel: 01273 777688
Fax: 01273 776755
info@viva.org.uk
www.viva.org.uk
Viva! (Vegetarians International
Voice for Animals) was launched
by the author of this book in
1994. It is an animal and vegetar-
ian/vegan charity with a special
section for under 18s. It produces
masses of free info on everything
from veggie recipes and nutrition
to saving animals and the planet.
Viva! actively campaigns against
factory farming, killing wild
animals for meat and skin,
slaughter and live exports.

Viva! also has free packs on
campaigning for veggie school
meals, how to Convert-a-Parent
and Schools' Campaign Opposed
to Factory Farming (SCOFF!).
Produces *Viva!Life* magazine and
a mini-mag for under 18s,
Vivactive!. Viva! has a penpal
service for young supporters as
well as youth contacts and adult
groups throughout the UK.

Whale and Dolphin Conservation Society (WDCS)
Alexander House
19a James Street West
Bath BA1 2BT
Tel: 01225 334511
Adoption hotline: 0870 870 5001
info@wdcs.org
www.wdcs.org
Dedicated to the protection of
cetaceans (whales, dolphins and
porpoises) and their environment. Runs a whale and dolphin
adoption scheme.

World Parrot Trust
Glanmor House
Hayle TR27 4HB
Tel: 01736 751026
uk@worldparrottrust.org
www.worldparrottrust.org
Conserves wild parrots and
works for more caring 'ownership' of captive birds.

World Society for the Protection
of Animals (WSPA)
14th Floor
89 Albert Embankment
London SE1 7TP
Tel: 020 7793 0540
wspa@wspa.org.uk
wspa.org.uk
Worldwide animal welfare group
running strong campaigns against
fur, cruelty to bears, hunting of
endangered species, bullfighting
and so on.

World Wildlife Fund (WWF)
Panda House
Weyside Park
Godalming GU7 1XR
Tel: 01483 426444
wwf-uk@wwf-uk.org
www.wwf.org
Conservation group (not animal
rights) active in 100 countries.
Helps fund wildlife reserves and
anti-poaching teams.

Zoo Check (see Born Free
Foundation)

USA

American Anti-Vivisection
Society (AAVS)
801 Old York Road, Suite 204
Jenkintown, PA 19046
Tel: 800 729 2287
Campaigns against experiments
on animals.

American Fund for Alternatives
to Animal Research (AFAAR)
175 West 12th Street, Suite 16G
New York, NY 10011–8275
Tel: 212 989 8073
Gives grants to develop non-
animal tests and publishes
findings of research.

American Vegan Society
PO Box H
Malaga, NJ 08328
Tel: 609 694 2887
Produces information on the
vegan diet and has extensive
book mailorder service.

The Animals' Agenda
3500 Boston Street, Suite 325
Baltimore, MD 21224
Tel: 410 675 4566
Subscriptions (US): 800 426 6884
office@animalsagenda.org
www.animalsagenda.org
Bimonthly animal-rights
magazine covering issues and
events in the US and UK.

Beauty Without Cruelty
175 West 12th Street, 16G
New York, NY 10011
Tel: 212 989 8073
International organisation
promoting alternatives to all
animal use.

Coalition to Abolish the Fur
Trade (CAFT)
PO Box 822411
Dallas, TX 75382
Tel: 214 503 1419
caft13@aol.com
www.banfur.com
Grassroots organisation dedicated
to abolishing the fur trade.

Doris Day Animal League (DDAL)
Suite 100
227 Massachusetts Ave, NE
Washington, DC 20002
Tel: 202 546 1761
www.ddal.org
The goal of DDAL is to pass laws
to reduce the suffering of animals
wherever they are mistreated.
Also helps draft legislation,
organise support and lobbying
for or against legislation in cities
across the US.

EarthSave International
1509 Seabright Avenue
Suite B1
Santa Cruz, CA 95062
Tel: 831 423 0293
Information@EarthSave.org
www.earthsave.org
Raises awareness of the ecologi-
cal destruction linked to the
production of farmed animals.
Helps people go vegan.

Farm Sanctuary
3100 Aikens Road

Watkins Glen, NY 14891
Tel: 530 865 4617
www.farmsanctuary.org
Works to prevent cruelty to
farmed animals through legislation, investigations, education and
direct rescue programmes. Runs
two sanctuaries for rescued
farmed animals. Promotes a
vegan lifestyle.

Friends of Animals (FoA)
777 Post Road, Suite 205
Darien, CT 06820
Tel: 203 656 1522
foa1@igc.org
www.friendsofanimals.org
International animal protection
organisation. Work includes anti-
poaching campaigns, educational
and legislative efforts to save
elephants and other wildlife. Pro-
vegetarian and anti-fur.

The Fund for Animals
200 West 57th Street
New York, NY 10019
Tel: 212 246 2096
fundinfo@fund.org
www.fund.org
Active group campaigning
against hunting and has used
lawsuits to stop many hunts of
wild animals. Opposes animals
kept in captivity, factory farming
and more. Also runs the Black
Beauty horse sanctuary in Texas.

Humane Farming Association
1550 California Street, Suite 6
San Francisco, CA 94109
Tel: 415 771 2253
Leads a national campaign to
stop factory farmers from
misusing chemicals and
abusing farmed animals.

Humane Society of the United
States (HSUS)
2100 L Street NW
Washington, DC 20037
Tel: 202 452 1100
www.hsus.org
Programmes focus on humane
education, wildlife protection,
farmed animals, companion
animals and animal-research
issues.

In Defense of Animals
131 Camino Alto, Suite E,
Mill Valley, CA 94941
Tel: 415 388 9641
ida@idausa.org
www.idausa.org
Animal-rights group fighting
against the fur and meat trades,
captive whales, vivisection and
more. Works through protest,
education and legal action to
advocate lifestyles and technolo-
gies that do not exploit animals.

Last Chance for Animals (LCA)
8033 Sunset Boulevard, #835
Los Angeles, CA 90046

Tel: 310 271 6096 or 888 88
ANIMAL
www.lcanimal.org
Anti-vivisection, anti-fur, direct-
action animal-rights organisation
that maintains an information
hotline regarding demonstrations
and events.

National Anti-Vivisection
Society (NAVS)
53 West Jackson Blvd, Suite 1552
Chicago, IL 60604 3795
Tel: 800 888 6287

The Nature of Wellness
PO Box 10400
Glendale, CA 91209–3400
Tel: 818 790 6384
Fax: 818 790 9660
www.animalresearch.org
Offers educational resources
concerning the use of animals in
research, the problems involved
and the alternatives.

North American Vegetarian
Society
PO Box 72
Dolgeville, NY 13329
Tel: 518 568 7970
navs@telenet.net
www.navs-online.org
Dedicated to the promotion
of vegetarianism through
education, publications and
annual conferences.

People for the Ethical Treatment
of Animals (PETA)
501 Front Street
Norfolk, VA 23510
Tel: 757 622 PETA (7382)
info@peta-online.org
www.peta-online.org
The USA's largest animal-rights
group actively campaigns against
all animal abuse, with many
successes. PETA has an education
department which is working to
stop dissection and has lots of
free youth materials covering
everything from the meat and
fur trades to anti-vivisection
and performing animals. PETA's
brilliant magazine, *Animal Times*,
is not to be missed!

Physicians Committee for
Responsible Medicine (PCRM)
5100 Wisconsin Avenue NW,
Suite 404
Washington, DC 20016
Tel: 202 686 2210
pcrm@pcrm.org
www.pcrm.org
Produces excellent info on why a
vegan diet is the healthiest on
Earth! Promotes preventive
medicine and ethical research.
Supported by 5000 physicians, as
well as lay folk.

Plenty International
PO Box 394

Summertown, TN 38483
plenty1@usit.net
www.plenty.org
Has worked with villages around
the world since 1979 to enhance
nutrition and local food self-
sufficiency through vegetarianism.

Progressive Animal Welfare
Society (PAWS)
PO Box 1037
Lynnwood, WA 98046
Tel: 425 787 2500
www.paws.org
Animal-advocacy and direct-care
organisation in the Pacific
Northwest. Their wildlife centre
is a world leader in wildlife rehabilitation; also runs a companion-
animal shelter and campaigns to
end animal exploitation and
cruelty.

SPAY USA
Tel: 800 248 SPAY (7729)
Helps people find low-cost
veterinarians in their local area.

Tattoo-A-Pet
6571 SW 20th Court
Fourt Lauderdale, FL 33317
Tel: 800 828 8667
Has about one million dogs
registered that are given a painless tattoo to identify them, with
2000 authorised facilities

nationwide. They claim a
99 per cent recovery rate.

United Poultry Concerns (UPC)
12325 Seaside Road
Machipongo, VA 23405
Tel: 757 678 7875
Uncovers the truth behind the
poultry industry with great
campaigns and information.

Vegan Action
PO Box 4353
Berkeley
California, CA 94704
Tel: 510 548 7377
www.vegan.org
Educational group promoting
veganism, with plenty of materials on animals, the environment
and health. Campaigns for the
increased availability of vegan
foods and produces a monthly
newsletter.

Vegan Outreach
211 Indian Drive
Pittsburgh, PA 15238
Tel: 412 968 0268
vegan@veganoutreach.org
veganoutreach.org
Educational group with info on
factory farming, slaughter, health
and help for people wanting to
change their diet.

Vegetarian Resource Group
PO Box 1463
Baltimore, MD 21203
Tel: 410 366 8343
vrg@vrg.org
www.vrg.org
Contact for plenty of info
on anything and everything
vegetarian. Produces a guide to
vegetarian restaurants in the USA.

Viva! (USA)
PO Box 49023
Atlanta, GA 30359
Tel: 404 315 8881
info@vivausa.org
www.vivausa.org
Viva! (Vegetarians International
Voice for Animals) was launched
by the author of this book in the
UK in 1994 and in the US in
2000. A dynamic animal rights
and vegetarian/vegan organisation with a special section for
under 18s. It produces masses of
free info on everything from
saving animals and the planet to
vegan recipes and nutrition. Viva!
actively campaigns against factory
farming, live exports, slaughter
and killing wild animals for meat
and skin. It also runs brilliant
education programmes.

VivaVegie Society
PO Box 294
Prince Street Station

New York, NY 10012
Tel: 212 414 9100
www.vivavegie.org
New York's vegetarian outreach
organisation with active programme of lectures and social
meetings. Encourages voluntary
help.

World Society for the Protection
of Animals – USA
29 Perkins Street
PO Box 190
Boston, MA 02130
Tel: 617 522 7000
Fax: 617 522 7077
wspa@wspausa.com
Worldwide animal welfare group
running strong campaigns against
fur, cruelty to bears, hunting of
endangered species, bullfighting
and so on.

World Watch Institute
1776 Massachusetts Avenue, NW
Washington, DC 20036–1904
Tel: 202 452 1999
worldwatch@worldwatch.org
www.worldwatch.org
Promotes a sustainable society by
researching global environmental
issues, the results of which are
widely disseminated throughout
the world. Produces bimonthly
World Watch magazine.

World Wildlife Fund – USA
1250 Twenty-Fourth Street, NW

PO Box 97180
Washington, DC 20037
Tel: 800 CALL WWF
www.wwf.org
Wildlife conservation group (not
animal rights) active in 100
countries. Helps fund wildlife
reserves and anti-poaching teams.

Youth for Environmental Sanity
(YES)
420 Bronco Road
Soquel, CA 95073–9510
Tel: 877 293 7226
camps@yesworld.org
www.camps@yesworld.org
Inspires young people to take
action for the planet.

Australia

Animal Liberation has branches
in all Australian states. It is run by
volunteers and promotes animal
rights. Focal campaigns are
against intensive farming and
animal experiments and for
humane education and wildlife
protection. Also operates a hands-
on investigation and rescue
department and the famous
'no-kill' 'Give A Dog A Home'
scheme.

Animal Liberation (ACT)
GPO Box 1875
Canberra City 2601

Tel: 06 247 48358

Animal Liberation (NSW)
535A King Street
Newtown
NSW 2042
Tel: 029 565 5484
sydneyhq@animal-lib.org.au
www.animal-lib.org.au

Animal Liberation (QLD)
131 Melbourne Street
South Brisbane
QLD 4101
Tel: 07 3844 5533
www.powerup.com.au/~alibqld
alibqld@powerup.com.au

Animal Liberation (SA)
PO Box 114
Rundle Mall
Adelaide SA 5000
www.animaliberation.org.au
animal.liberation.sa@picknowl.
com.au

Animal Liberation (TAS) Inc
Environment Centre
102 Bathurst Street
Hobart
Tasmania 7000
Tel: 02 345 543

Animal Liberation (VIC)
88A Smith Street
Collingwood
Victoria 3066

Tel: 03 9419 5188
alibvic@animalib.org.au
http://home.vicnet.net.au/
-animalib/

Animal Liberation (WA)
PO Box 8173
Perth
WA 6849
Tel: 08 9225 4101
alwa@iinet.net.au

Animals Australia
37 O'Connell Street
North Melbourne
Melbourne
Victoria 3051
Tel: 03 9329 6333
animals@melbpc.org.au
An umbrella group with 40
animal group members. Has extensive research and information
on all areas of animals abuse, from
the kangaroo massacre to banning battery-hen cages. Produces
Animals Today magazine.

Australian Association for
Humane Research
PO Box 779
Darlinghurst
NSW 1300
Promotes all viable methods of
healing which do not involve the
use of animals and works for the
abolition of all experiments using
animals.

Australian Wildlife Protection
Council
Ross House
247 Flinders Lane
Melbourne
Victoria 3000
Tel: 03 9650 8326
kangaroo@peninsula.hotkey.net.
au
www.geocities.com/awpc
Active lobbying to save the
kangaroo and other wildlife.
Produced excellent book, *The
Kangaroo Betrayed*, to help stop
the largest land wildlife massacre
on Earth.

Compassion for Animals (WA)
PO Box 1608
Morley
WA 6943
New anti-vivisection group.

Guardians
PO Box 59
Pascoe Vale
Victoria 3778
guardians@werple.net.au
Exposes the horrors and risks of
vivisection.

Humane Society International
PO Box 302
Avalon
NSW 2107
General animal-rights group with
main focus against vivisection.

International Fund for Animals
Welfare (IFAW)
PO Box 448
Artarmon
NSW 2064
Tel: 02 668 72252
www.ifaw.org
Campaigns against all animal
abuse.

New Vegetarian and Natural Health
PO Box 65
Paddington
NSW 2021
Tel: (editorial) 02 9698 4339
avs@primus.com.au
Quarterly magazine which
focuses on vegetarian and vegan
nutrition and health issues but
also explores animal and ecological areas. Sent to supporters of
the various Vegetarian Societies
and available on news-stands.

People Against Cruelty in Animal
Transport (PACAT)
PO Box 152
South Gremantle
WA 6162
Tel: 08 9377 0781
Active group which works to
ban live exports.

There are several vegetarian and
vegan groups promoting a
cruelty-free way of life:

Vegan Society (NSW)
PO Box 467
Broadway
NSW 2007
Tel/Fax: 02 9436 1373
www.vegansociety.com

Australian Vegetarian Society (ACT)
PO Box 1786
Canberra Act 2601
Tel/Fax: 02 6258 6632
dambiec@ozemail.com.au
www.moreinfo.com.au/aus/

Australian Vegetarian Society (TAS)
PO Box 74
Bicheno
Tasmania 7215
Tel: 03 6375 1829
www.moreinfo.com.au/aus/

Vegetarian Network Victoria
GPO Box 2633X
Melbourne
Victoria 3001
Tel: 0500-VEGIES
www.vnv.org.au

Vegetarian/Vegan Society of
Queensland
1086 Waterworks Road
The Gap
Queensland 4061
Tel: 07 3300 9320
www.angelfire.com/az/vvsq/

Vegetarian Society of South
Australia
PO Box 46
Rundle Mall

Adelaide
SA 5000
Tel: 08 8261 3194

Vegetarian Society of Western
Australia
PO Box 220
North Perth
WA 6906
Tel/Fax: 08 9275 5682
wsq@bigfoot.com
www.vswa@ivu.org

World League for the Protection
of Animals
PO Box 211
Gladesville
NSW 2111
Strong campaigns to stop cruelty
to companion animals and on anti-
vivisection; works to end the practice of sending pound animals for
research in NSW.

World Society for the Protection
of Animals – Australia
46 Nicholson Street
St Leonards
NSW 2065
Tel: 02 9901 5205
Fax: 02 9906 7703
wspa@ozemail.com.au
wspa.org.uk
Worldwide animal-welfare group
running strong campaigns against
fur, cruelty to bears, hunting of endangered species, bullfighting etc.

Index

alligators 18
angling 173–84
animal experiments 83–98
    alternatives to 93
    Draize test 87
    history of 90–1
    ineffectiveness of 88–90, 93–4
    and new drugs 88–9, 91–3
    'toxicity testing' 86, 95–6
animals
    domestication of 126
    role of 232–3
antelope 36
antibiotics 127, 183, 235
arctic fox 9
auks 37

badgers 10, 28, 29, 234
beagles 84, 87
beak trimming 135, 136, 138
bears
    bear baiting 28, 211
    and Chinese medicine 51–2
    in circuses 72
    hunting 10, 37, 38, 42
    in zoos 68

beavers 10, 11, 12
Belgian Blue cows 192–3
Beltsville pig 193–4
bighorn sheep 37
birds
    caged 66, 114–15
    hunting 33–4, 36, 38, 234
    protected 2, 34
    returning to wild 118
bison 25–6, 37
blow torches 165
blue whale 48
boars 36
bobcats 36, 38
BSE (bovine spongiform
    encephalopathy) 141, 151
BST (bovine somatotrophin) 194–6
Buddhism, and vegetarianism 202,
    203–4, 211
bulls
    bullfighting 39–41
    live export 154
    ritual slaughter 207–8
bushmeat 224, 226, 227

camels 72

Canada geese 34
captive bolt pistol 156, 158
carbon dioxide
    gas stunning 137, 159–60
    and global warming 237
carbon monoxide poisoning 15
cats
    as companions 110–12
    for meat 166
    selective breeding 104
    wild 12–13, 68
cattle
    genetic engineering 191–3
    growth hormones 194–5
    live export 151, 153–4
    milk production 140–2, 194–5
    ritual slaughter 162–3
    slaughter 16–17, 158
cheetahs 4–5, 12
chickens
    egg production 133–7
    factory farming 126, 127,
        131–33
    genetic engineering 194
    male chicks 136
    origins of 133
    slaughter 158–9
chimpanzees 69, 72, 73–4, 215–17
Chinese medicine 51, 219, 220–1,
    223
Christianity 206–8
circuses 72–4, 78
cloning 197–8
coarse fishing 173–4, 177–9
cock fighting 28
cod 180, 185
companion animals 101–21
    if you see cruelty to 120–1
    from rescue centres 106, 117
    pet shops 106
conibear trap 11–12
cormorants 178–9

cougars 36, 38
coyotes 36, 232
crocodiles 18
crows 2, 234

Darwin, Charles 71–2
deer 35, 36, 38
dioxins 180
'disgorger' 174–5
dog fighting 28
dogs
    in animal experiments 84, 87,
        89–90
    as companions 107–10, 117
    as guard dogs 101–2
    and hunting 32–3, 35, 38
    for meat 165–6, 167
    puppy farms 118
    selective breeding 103–4
    skin 17, 18
dolphins 48, 50, 74–7, 182, 235,
    237
donkeys 207
doves 36, 38
drift nets 181–2, 185
ducks 2, 34, 36
    factory farming 137–8, 143
eagles 37
electric goads 153, 154
electric tongs 156–6
electrified water bath 156, 158–9
electrocution 15, 156–7, 165
elephants 3–4, 45–6, 52–3, 60–1
    in circuses 72, 74
    in zoos 70–1
elk 36
extinction 6, 12, 115, 217–29, 238
    habitat destruction 37, 219, 223
    hunting 26, 37, 48, 49–50,
        219–21, 224

factory farming 66, 122–43, 183–4

antibiotics 127, 132
farming
   efficiency 232–3
   intensive 237
fish
   as companions 116
   declining stocks 58, 180, 183, 185
   factory farming 183–4
   and pain 172–3, 179
   and ultraviolet light 236
fishing 171–84
   angling 173–9
   damage by hook 174–5, 178
   industrialised 179–83
   and litter 175–6
   live bait 175
   traditional methods 179
food-poisoning 127
foxes 9, 10, 14, 15, 28, 29, 38
foxhunting 23–5, 27–33
   cubbing 33
   excuses for 28, 30–3, 36, 234
   terriermen 29–30
fur farming 14–15

game fishing 173–4
gas stunning 156, 159–60
geese 34, 36
genetic engineering 187–200
   and animals 191–9
   opposition to 199
   and plants 190–1
Geoffroy's cat 12
global warming 237
goats 163, 207, 212–3
gorillas 224–7, 229, 238
   sold for meat 114, 226
   in zoos 68, 69
grouse 34, 234

hawks 234

heath hen 37
hedgerows 233
Hindu religion 211–12
horses 112–14
   and bullfighting 40
   in circuses 72
   racehorses 112–13
   selective breeding 112, 113
   transporting 17–18
   wild 53
hounds 32–3
hunting 22–38, 234–5
   excuses for 34, 36, 38, 55, 58
   extinction 26, 37, 48, 49–50, 219–21, 224
   and profit 59–60

insects 232, 233
ivory 45–6, 52–3

jaguars 12
Jews
   ritual slaughter 162, 163–5, 208
   and vegetarianism 208–9

kangaroos 53–7, 60
   'joeys' 54, 56
   methods of killing 55–6
   skin 17, 56

'lairage' 156
leather 15–18
   alternatives 19–20
leghold traps 10–11, 19
leopards 12
lions 72
live-export trade 149–55, 166–7
llamas 72
lynx 10, 12, 38

'mad cow disease' 141, 151
magpies 2, 234

mangrove swamps 184
margays 12
marmosets 70
meat production *see* factory
    farming
medicines 59, 196–7
minke whales 50
mink 10, 11, 14, 15, 20, 35
mole rats 4
monkeys 87–8, 97
moon bears 51–2
moose 36
muskrats 11
Muslim religion
    compassion for animals 210–11,
        212
    ritual slaughter 149–50, 162,
        163–5
    and vegetarianism 210

natural selection 5, 57

ocelots 12
orcas (killer whales) 74
organ transplantation 196
ostriches 18
otters 10, 34, 184
overfishing 50, 180, 237
owls 234
ozone layer 236, 237

panthers 37
partridges 2, 25, 34
PCBs 180
pesticides and herbicides 233–4
pets *see* companion animals
pharmaceutical companies
    animal experiments 91–2
    genetic engineering 189
pheasants 2, 25, 34, 36, 234
pigeons 26, 37, 38, 234

pigs
    factory farming 123–4, 126,
        127–31, 143
    genetic engineering 193–4
    leather 16
    live export 153
    organ transplantation 195–6
    slaughter 156, 159–60, 161
pilot whales 51
poisoned darts 53
polar bears 69
pollution 180, 233–4, 236
pony skin 17–18
porpoises 48, 182
poultry
    ritual slaughter 163
    see also chickens
prairie dogs 38, 232
prawns (shrimps) 166, 184
pronghorn antelope 36
purse seine nets 182

quail 36, 37

rabbits 36, 234
    in animal experiments 87
    as companions 116–17
    selective breeding 104
racoons 10, 12, 38
rainforest, destruction of 217, 227,
    238
rats and mice 89, 234
religion
    and animals 149–50, 151,
        202–13
    and vegetarianism 206–12
rhinos 221–4, 228, 238
ritual slaughter 149–50, 151, 155,
    162–5, 167, 207
rooks 2, 234

sable 10

salmon, colouring 183
sea fishing 173, 176–7
sea minks 12
sea otters 12
seabirds 183, 184, 237
seals 57–60, 183, 184, 235, 237
    cubs 58–9
selective breeding 103–4, 112, 113, 235
sheep
    breeding cycle 139
    farming methods 138–40
    genetic engineering 193, 196
    leather 16
    live export 149–50, 151–3
    ritual slaughter 149–50, 151, 163
    slaughter of 161–2
    wool production 139–40
slaughter 155–67
    boiling alive 166
    efficiency 155, 158
    and live export 153
    methods of 156–66
    ritual 149–50, 151, 155, 162–5, 167, 207
    skinning alive 18
slaughterhouses, and cruelty 153, 160–2
snakes 18
snares 11, 12, 53
snipe 2
snow leopards 12, 13
sperm whales 48

squirrels 10, 36
superbugs 127, 235
swans 36, 176
Swiss Brown cows 193

terriers 29–30
tigers 25, 218–21, 227–8, 238, 239
    in circuses 72
    cubs 219–20, 227–8
    in zoos 69
Tompson's gazelles 4–5
'trash' animals 12
trawling 181
tuna 182
turkeys 36, 158–9

ultraviolet light 236–7
underwater traps 11

veal production 141–2, 151
vegetarianism 125, 126, 142
    and religion 163, 165, 202, 203–4, 206–12
vivisection see animal experiments

wallabies 70
whales 47–51, 61–2, 182, 234, 239
wolves 10, 12, 36, 37, 42
woodcocks 2, 25, 34

zoos 65–72, 77–8
    breeding programmes 67–8
    'stereotypic behaviour' 69

If you don't want this little piggie to go to market...

support *Viva!*

Why *Viva!*?
Every year in Britain more than 800 million animals face the barbarity of slaughter – many fully conscious. Most spend their short lives in confinement, pain and misery.

Every year, the earth staggers closer to environmental disaster. Whether polluted water or torched forests, eroded topsoil or spreading deserts – livestock production is at the heart of the problem. Overfishing is having an equally devastating effect on the world's oceans.

Every year, millions of people in the developing world die from hunger – alongside fields of fodder destined for the West's livestock.

Every year, proof increases that vegetarians are healthier than meat eaters.

Overnight, with the simple decision to stop eating meat and fish, you cease to play a part in this insanity.

Saving Animals
With regular, hard-hitting campaigns, *Viva!* saves lives and ends suffering.

For a free pack on saving animals – which includes a colour poster, leaflets and petition forms – send your name and address to *Viva!*.

Going Veggie
And if you're a learner veggie – or thinking of becoming one – *Viva!* is here to help. Contact us for a free Going Veggie pack. For guides on what foods are easily available, buy the *L-Plate Vegetarian* or *L-Plate Vegan* (£1 each including p&p). *Viva!* has a great range of other guides on everything veggie, including health, nutrition, the environment, sports health, recipes... send for the list.

Join *Viva!*
To join the best group in the cosmos (probably), just send *Viva!* a cheque for £5 (if under 18) or £15 (if 18 or over) with your name, age and address. (UK only – for EU add 50%, elsewhere add 100%). You'll receive special stickers, posters, leaflets and four issues of our great colour mag, *Viva!Life*, plus *Viva!Active* – a special pull-out colour section for young supporters. **Join the fight for life – support *Viva!***

Viva!, 12 Queen Square, Brighton BN1 3FD. Tel: 01273 777688
E: info@viva.org.uk W: www.viva.org.uk

Registered Charity 1037486